The
LAWSUIT
LOTTERY
THE HIJACKING OF JUSTICE IN AMERICA

The LAWSUIT LOTTERY

THE HIJACKING OF JUSTICE IN AMERICA

Douglass S. Lodmell, J.D., LL.M.
Benjamin R. Lodmell

WORLD CONNECTION
PUBLISHING
Phoenix, Arizona

Disclaimer
The purpose of information detailed in this book is to provide accurate and authoritative information regarding the subject matter covered and not to render specific legal, accounting or tax advice. For specific advice geared to your specific situation, please consult a licensed expert.

Contents

Acknowledgements

First and foremost, we would like to thank Bill Moran, who spent over two years studying from the inside out the many problems associated with the U.S. tort system and *"the lawsuit lottery,"* (a phrase aptly coined by University of Virginia law professor Jeffrey O'Connell). The final form of this book could not have been achieved without his extensive research, insight and extensive editorial contributions.

We also want to express our gratitude to Walter K. Olson, Grant Gilmore and Philip K. Howard, whose scholarly opinions and collective writings helped inspire and light the way for this social commentary.

Our thanks also goes to the Tillinghast Division of Towers Perrin, whose unique historical statistical data on the cost of the U.S. tort system helped in assessing the *ultimate* cost of the litigation craze on the character of America and Americans.

We are also indebted to those many friends and colleagues who read the manuscript and offered important critical advice and suggestions.

Finally, we want to acknowledge the singular importance of our family: our dad and first mentor, Gary L. Lodmell, J.D., whose lifelong respect for the-law-as-the-law-was-intended and his unstinting support and moral guidance made this commentary possible; our mother, Jannette Edwards, who has always been our personal walking library and a great source of inspiration and support; and our second father, Melvin Edwards, who, better than anyone else, has provided us with a living example of what taking personal responsibility in life really means.

About the Authors

■ **Douglass S. Lodmell, J.D., LL.M.**
Co-founder/Managing Partner
Lodmell & Lodmell, P.C., Phoenix, AZ
Co-founder: World Children's Relief & Volunteer Organization,
Inc., Phoenix, AZ

Born in Geneva, Switzerland, in 1968, Douglass Lodmell was raised and educated in the United States, where he followed his father's footsteps into the legal profession, becoming an attorney and a nationally renowned expert in asset protection law, international trusts and estate planning.

He earned a Bachelor of Science Degree in finance from the University of Northern Colorado and a Juris Doctorate, *Magna Cum Laude,* from Benjamin Cardozo School of Law at Yeshiva University in New York. While attending the Cardozo School of Law, he was awarded the prestigious Jacob Burns Medal for scholastic achievement. Douglass went on to receive an LL.M. Degree in taxation at New York University School of Law.

While in law school, Douglass was privileged to serve as Law Clerk to the Honorable Judge Jack Weinstein of the U.S. District Court of the Eastern District of New York.

With his father, long-time estate planning attorney Gary L. Lodmell, J.D., Douglass co-founded and is Managing Partner of Lodmell & Lodmell, P.C. in Phoenix, Arizona.

With a nationwide client base of more than 3,000 healthcare and business professionals, Lodmell & Lodmell is one of the country's few law firms practicing exclusively in the field of estate planning and asset protection.

As an expert in asset protection, Douglass has authored numerous articles for professional journals and is a frequent guest speaker on the subject of how to safeguard wealth in an increasingly litigious society. *The Lawsuit Lottery…The Hijacking of Justice in America!* is his first book.

■ Benjamin R. Lodmell

Director of Business Development:
Lodmell & Lodmell, P.C., Phoenix, AZ
Co-founder/Executive Director: World Children's Relief & Volunteer Organization, Inc., Phoenix, AZ

Benjamin Lodmell was born in Phoenix, Arizona, into a lawyer's family. Unlike his older brother, Douglass, who became an expert in asset protection law, or his father, Gary, who has been practicing business law and estate planning for more than 35 years, Benjamin chose a career path in business and international affairs.

That career path eventually would involve him in the 1997 start-up and development of the family law firm and, with Douglass, the establishment and operation of an international non-profit charity—World Children's Relief & Volunteer Organization.

At Connecticut College, Benjamin earned a Bachelor of Arts Degree in economics and international relations. He spent a summer in Lima, Peru, as a Fellow at the Center for International Studies in the Liberal Arts as an assistant to Director Hernando De Soto.

During college, Ben studied European Union economics at the University of Seville in Spain.

Prior to joining Lodmell & Lodmell in 1997 as director of business development, he held executive positions with the Federal Reserve Bank, Chemical Bank, Credit Lyonnais, and Merrill Lynch.

Currently, Ben spends most of his time traveling throughout the developing world as executive director of World Children's Relief & Volunteer Organization, Inc., a non-profit charity dedicated to providing real hope through education to children in some of the world's poorest countries.

Dedication

This book is dedicated to
Hawah Foryoh, Hawa Bockarie, Lucinda Bangalie,
Mary Sesay, Zainab Kanu and Ballay Kargbo.
Your courage is an inspiration to us
and we love you with all our hearts.

Introduction

There was a brief moment when we considered dedicating this book to William Shakespeare. That's when we were reminded that, 400 years ago, the Bard of Avon penned his famous line about killing all the lawyers.

Shakespeare wrote that line in *Henry VI, Part II.* Quote it now—as it is on many occasions at conferences and seminars—and you likely will get a good laugh from the audience and a few nods of agreement from lawyers who doubtlessly have heard it many times before.

Ironically, when we think about Shakespeare's words today, they conjure up a meaning very different from what the author meant to convey when those words were spoken for the first time.

In Shakespeare's play, the character "Dick, the butcher" suggests killing "all the lawyers" not because they were bad guys but because, once upon a time, the public's perception of lawyers was that they stood for justice and argued the law—something "Dick the butcher" and his cronies could not tolerate in Shakespeare's play. My, how the times, they have changed!

Our guess is that today's anti-lawyer cynicism and derisive jokes are as plentiful and unflattering as any time in history, perhaps more so in this litigious society of ours.

Paradoxically, the public's generally negative perception of lawyers seems to persist despite the evolutionary improvement in the legal profession's *functional* value to society.

Today you hear the anti-lawyer cynicism in movies. You encounter it on radio and television. You read it in books and newspapers. There's no end to the jokes, such as: "What do you call 1,000 lawyers chained under the ocean?" "A good beginning!" Or, "What's the difference between a lawyer and a vulture?" "Lawyers can take off their wingtips!"

Some anti-lawyer jokes are even more pointed in their cynicism, such as in Carl Sandburg's "The People, Yes." There, when America's Pulitzer Prize winning poet-author asks, "Have you a criminal lawyer in this burg?" the reply is, "We think so, but we haven't been able to prove it on him yet."

Although lawyers have been the subject of jokes for centuries —if not millennia—the reasons behind the public attitudes prompting such ill-humor have changed with the times. This book examines the more recent changes and the depth of the feelings behind them.

While much has been written about the unrelenting amount of litigation in America, news media coverage tends to focus on the big-dollar lawsuits—those that drive giant corporations into bankruptcy and put thousands out of work, or the oddball court cases that make for silly headlines and titillating reading, or the powerful trial lawyers who get rich and richer by driving the litigation bandwagon to record highs year after year.

The harsh reality is that many if not most of the estimated 70,000 lawsuits filed every day in America target small business owners and mid-to-upper income Americans with less than $1-million in net worth. And not much is being written about that.

Nor has much been written about the trillions of litigation dollars that have been extracted as a "hidden tax" from the U.S. economy during the past several decades or the substantial social and political consequences the nation has suffered from being the world's most litigious society.

This book attempts to shed light on trends within the U.S. civil justice system that are spreading like an insidious cancer throughout society. It is a book written by those close enough to the subject's inner workings to write about it with sufficient knowledge and experience, yet far enough away from the system's vested interests to be objective about its consequences.

It is a book about how the world's costliest tort system is redistributing much of the nation's wealth from those who have it, to a growing society of self-proclaimed "victims" who want it and believe they are "entitled" to it.

It is a book about the resulting harm being inflicted on the nation's economy and infrastructure, the character of its people, and the legitimacy of a country once respected and, to some degree, envied by much of the world.

The book's intent is to draw public, legal and legislative attention to the far-reaching dangers posed by a continuation of the adverse trends at work in today's dysfunctional U.S. tort system.

An equally important goal is to help instigate suggested reforms, which, if ignored, may impose economic and social consequences well beyond the substantial damage already inflicted on the American people and the nation as a whole.

This is not intended to be a scholarly treatise on the "whys and wherefores" of the rise and fall of the U.S. tort system; we leave that to professors of law and legal scholars. They are the ones responsible for ensuring that tomorrow's lawyers understand what is right and wrong with our legal system so they can fix what needs fixing when they come of age.

Nor is this a book about the law as a profession. Nor is it a critique of *all* lawyers, or *all* judges, nor even most of them.

Rather, this is a social commentary—an extended essay, if you will, on a civil justice system that has been stealthily transformed from one that abhorred lawsuits into what is arguably the best-oiled and most costly litigation machine in the world.

Relying heavily on industry statistics, scholarly opinions, news reports, and other documentary evidence, *The Lawsuit Lottery* describes how a growing breed of entrepreneurial attorneys abuses the original purposes of the U.S. tort system by stirring up litigation that caters unashamedly to the public's selfish sense of victimization.

Because of the highly polarized debate between opponents and proponents of freewheeling litigation in America, separating reality from competing rhetoric regarding the ultimate cost of the burgeoning U.S. tort system has been daunting, to say the least.

To avoid confusing the reader with often conflicting and widely-varying news media reports on the cost of torts, the Tillinghast Division of Towers Perrin was selected as the book's primary statistical source. This choice was made for three reasons: First, Tillinghast is one of the world's leading independent actuarial consultants to the financial services industry. Second, Tillinghast has been collecting tort cost data longer than any other statistical source (its analysis, which began in 1985, dates back to 1950). Third, and perhaps most importantly, Tillinghast's data offers the most comprehensive tort cost information available, providing a more coherent and consistent picture of the cost of litigation in America.

This book chronicles how predator-attorneys have vested interests in the financial outcome of litigation and how they encourage the unhealthy sense of entitlement that percolates today in every corner of American society by promising everyone with a gripe a chance to get rich quick at someone else's expense in the game called *the lawsuit lottery.*

This book questions the abusive practices of those attorneys who have acquired inordinate power and riches by convincing the courts that litigation is good—much to the detriment of America.

The book puts into layman's perspective:

- How hundreds of billions of dollars a year are being extracted from the U.S. economy—much of it by legal "extortion;"
- How the astronomical and spiraling cost of litigation is harming America's infrastructure;
- How a plaintiff-friendly tort system is immobilizing risk-taking in America by making citizens fearful of a legal system they once revered; and
- How a much-abused and dysfunctional civil justice system is contributing to the decline of America's moral leadership and legitimacy.

The book suggests ways to fix a flawed legal system whose once protective shield has been re-fashioned into a sword that threatens us all.

Given the nature of the opinions expressed and the ownership of the oxen being gored herein, it should not be surprising that challenges to this social commentary may emerge, particularly among trial attorneys.

In response to any such criticism, we would paraphrase the words of George Bernard Shaw, who suggested that when confronted by truth some might at first confuse it with blasphemy. So be it.

Some might even ponder why an asset protection attorney would challenge the basis for his own livelihood. The reason is that our civil justice system is no longer civil or just.

That's not the reason we established an asset protection law firm, however. About a dozen years ago, while I was in law school and Ben was engaged in international banking, we decided that helping clients to legally shield their hard-earned wealth from frivolous and indiscriminate lawsuits would be a great opportunity for the practice of law. And we were right. (A detailed explanation of asset protection planning appears later in the book).

What we didn't anticipate at the time was just how flawed and exorbitantly costly the U.S. tort system would become, or how devastating the consequences of the *lawsuit lottery* would be for Americans and America, or how imperative would be the reforms recommended in this book.

Do away with the worst elements of the U.S. tort system, as suggested in the book's final chapter, and the need for asset protection will likewise melt away—along with the public's growing fear of the law.

Then maybe—*maybe then*—the backhanded humor sparked to some extent by Shakespeare four centuries ago also will disappear.

Until then, however, did you hear the one about the guy who walked into a bar, leading an alligator by a leash? "Do you serve lawyers here?" the guy asked. "Sure do," the bartender replied. "Good. Then give me a beer and a lawyer for my 'gator."

Chapter 1

...The Law's Transformation

"All great truths begin as blasphemies."

— George Bernard Shaw (1856–1950)
Irish dramatist-critic

With an estimated 70,000 civil lawsuits every day and a million attorneys—more than any other country in the world—America may be "enjoying" too much justice in the world's most litigious society.

French dramatist Jean Racine warned about the consequences of too much justice 340 years ago, when he wrote, "Extreme justice is often injustice." Two hundred years later, British Prime Minister William Gladstone expanded on Racine's warning by suggesting that, "National injustice is the surest road to national downfall."

Whether America's civil justice system finds itself sliding down the slippery slope to injustice is certainly arguable. The huge and escalating cost of the nation's out-of-control tort system speaks for itself: an estimated $233.4 billion in 2002 alone, with the expectation that annual tort costs will skyrocket to as much as $298.1 billion by 2005. That's the equivalent of about $1,003 for every man, woman and child in America. Think about it! The cost of civil litigation in America equates to about as much as Sweden's gross domestic product, twice the GDP of Ireland, and three times that of New Zealand!

If the exorbitant out-of-pocket cost of lawsuits for personal injury and other wrongful acts fails to cause extreme apprehension about the direction the U.S. legal system is moving, consider the adverse impact the proliferation of litigation has had on the character of Americans doing the suing as well as those who fear being sued as well as the palor of hostile and counter-productive emoticon and negative energy that is a natural byproduct of an adversarial proceeding. Add to that the resulting negative perception the world has of America's once-vaunted legitimacy, and one could easily conclude that lawsuit-happy America is in big trouble.

There was a time, however, and not too long ago, when America's judges and lawmakers almost universally viewed litigation as a pariah. In those days, our Common Law tradition discouraged the urge to sue; Americans turned to litigation only as a last resort. There used to be a stigma attached to "going to court," regardless of the reason.

Even Abraham Lincoln, a lawyer by trade, urged fellow lawyers to discourage litigation, despite the lure of money to be made by it. "Persuade your neighbors to compromise whenever you can," he advised his colleagues, adding cynically, "There will still be business enough."

In the past, when America was a meritocracy, people sensed what the law allowed and didn't allow. Citizens felt accountable for their choices and took responsibility for their actions. They accepted risks they wouldn't take today—not with the present fear of potential liability that threatens every individual decision and activity.

The public's past antipathy about going to court tended to dampen the demand side of litigation. What kept the supply side largely in check was the American Bar Association's now-defunct rules that forbade lawyers from instigating lawsuits.

Even so, the number of lawsuits in America increased gradually until 1977, when the Bar's *Rules of Professional Conduct* of the litigation road changed abruptly. That's when the Supreme Court gave its blessing to anyone with an urge to sue.

By giving lawyers the right to advertise for clients, the highest court in the land opened the floodgates to litigation by energizing the pursuit of "the great god buck" that drives much of the law business today.

Thus began the transformation of America's once-laudable tort system for the redress of civil grievances into what now amounts to little more than a get-rich-quick national lottery— where everybody plays, like it or not.

Why is it that the public once sensed the do's and don'ts of civil law—but not anymore? Why do people who once trusted the law now feel threatened by it? Perhaps an answer can be found in understanding what the law was like then—before *the lawsuit lottery* became a national pastime.

Perhaps the law was as simple then as professor Chester Smith, at the University of Arizona, explained a generation or so ago to our father Gary's class of would-be attorneys: "If it sounds fair and reasonable, it's probably the law. And if it ain't, then it ought to be the law."

That was then, and this is now. And the difference between

the two reflects a sea of change in the law and the public's attitude toward it.

CHANGING RULES

A couple of generations ago people believed they understood the law's ground rules and abided by them. What was thought to be fair and reasonable guided public behavior. Oh, what a liberating time that must have been!

But the rules have changed.

Reversing 200 years of tradition, the courts now bless the public's right to sue. Driven by a greedy system, greedy lawyers and the public's growing sense of victimization and entitlement, Americans have taken to litigation like fleas to a hound dog. As a result, the cost of torts in America has zoomed a *hundred fold* in a half-century. That's a growth rate almost three times faster than the national economy.

Chances are that Racine and Gladstone would be shocked by the amount of "justice" we dispense in America today, and even more shocked by the amount of *injustice* accompanying it.

Has the litigation landslide brought us to a better world, as the proponents of "suing for dollars" predicted? Judge for yourself. The huge financial cost alone would appear to greatly outweigh the relative value of the social benefits derived from providing easy access to today's U.S. tort system.

Consider that less than half of the hundreds of billions of dollars a year extracted from the national economy by litigation actually reaches those for whom it was intended and less than half of that compensates plaintiffs for actual damages.

Conversely, most of today's wildly irrational judgments and

settlements go to lawyers and other costs of litigation—a fact that may have prompted the following bit of anti-lawyer cynicism: "How can I ever thank you?" gushed a woman to the attorney who solved her legal problems. "My dear woman," the lawyer replied, "ever since the Phoenicians invented money there has been only one answer to that question."

EARLY AMERICAN LAW

One need not look far back to find a time when America possessed one of the most envied justice systems in the world. That reputation didn't come easily or overnight; we began earning it more than 200 years ago.

With recordkeeping as skimpy as it was at the start of the 17th century, we can surmise that American Law began soon after the first English colonists settled in Jamestown, Virginia, in 1607. Thirteen years later, the Plymouth Rock Pilgrims signed one of the earliest legal documents written by the colonists—*without* a lawyer, we hasten to add.

The Pilgrims called it the "Mayflower Compact," named after the ship that brought them from England in search of religious freedom. That short, simple document bound the settlers "... into a civil Body Politick, for our better Ordering and Preservation..." It also bound them to "... enact, constitute, and frame, such just and equal Laws, Ordinances, Acts, Constitutions, and Officers, from time to time, as shall be thought most meet and convenient for the general good of the Colony; unto which we promise all due Submission and Obedience."

As might be expected, pre-Revolutionary War courts in America reflected the authority of England and English Law. As in England, punishments in the colonies were swift, harsh, and meted out by judges with little if any legal training, most being farmers and merchants, with scant time for their legal duties.

Thus the roots of American Law were planted with seeds dating to the origins of English Law itself and to Roman law before that. A case could also be made that the law, as a concept, is as old as society itself.

Ever since people lived in some form of community, regardless of how small or primitive, *somebody*—or some entity—had responsibility for maintaining order and settling disputes. Which means there have always been courts and judges of one sort or another—as well as lawyers to argue the merits of disputes, presumably for a fee. Some things never change.

With that perspective in mind, it shouldn't be surprising that anti-lawyer cynics would contend that, "Lawyering is the world's oldest profession—despite claims to the contrary by other more forthright professionals."

Cynicism aside, the earliest stirrings of organized life undoubtedly contributed embryos of law that evolved over millennia into the complex judicial systems, theories and precedents referred to as *The Rule of Law.*

The Rule of Law is what gives government legitimacy. And it is the very foundation—the bedrock, if you will, upon which liberty and justice are based in America.

Far from a gradual process with a steady, linear progression, English Law—on which American Law was based initially—grew in dramatic fits and starts, as jurists adapted the law to the evolutionary and sometimes revolutionary changes in society.

Early English Common Law was nothing if not confusing and chaotic. Almost since its beginnings, English Law employed a neutral judge and a jury of peers to decide disputes based on a framework of predefined ideas. These ideas, over time and with repeated acceptance, became established law.

Rather than codifying legal decisions for future judicial guidance, English courts adopted a "Common Sense" approach and a "Reasonable Man" attitude toward resolving different types of disputes. This resulted in an ever-evolving Common Law that reflected changing times as well as the needs of the people served.

In addition to Common Law, English courts enforced Statutory Law and a criminal code for maintaining public order and control. But it was the common law that saw most of the action. Civil disputes, injuries and contracts fell under its domain.

Not until the 16th century, however, did England begin the slow process of producing a coherent system of jurisprudence.

As new types of legal disputes emerged, so did opportunities for development of the law. For added flexibility, English judges based decisions on the "Court of Law" or the "Court of Equity," as they saw fit.

In the "Court of Law," English judges relied on previous court decisions and legal principles, applying them to current cases. The main job of lawyers was to research the common law and argue how a client's position was consistent with previous court decisions. Winning arguments resulted in court decisions that added precedents to the body of law surrounding those issues for the courts' guidance in resolving future cases.

Unlike the Court of Law, the Court of Equity allowed judges to disregard common law if a decision would be unfair or opposed to the spirit of the law. By way of example, a "Court of Equity" would likely deem it unfair for someone convicted of killing a spouse to collect on that spouse's life insurance policy, even if the policy or the law failed to preclude it.

Although the courts of law and equity no longer exist as

separate courtrooms, the concepts continue to be applied by today's judges.

Having authority to decide cases based on fairness can be powerful judicial tool, especially when a "Court of Law" might point a decision in another direction.

LAW AS SCIENCE

By the 17th century, written collections of "Case Law" began appearing in England, bringing some semblance of order to Common Law, enabling its theoretical study.

It was during the 17th and 18th centuries—The Age of Enlightenment—that the "science" of Common Law and jurisprudence emerged, along with a whole range of other social sciences, including history, economics and sociology.

It was a time of growing enthusiasm and a shared belief in the inevitability of progress—a powerfully productive attitude that continues to this day throughout the industrialized world.

Not until the mid-18th century, however, did the great English jurist and scholar Sir William Blackstone "reduce to order and lucidity" what previously had been a formless mass of English case law.

Blackstone's *Commentaries on the Laws of England* exerted tremendous influence not only on the practice of law in England at the time but also on the adaptation of English Common Law in America.

Blackstone believed the theories of law he created were immutable and should be relied upon for future court decisions. Not everyone agreed.

As Blackstone looked to the past to structure future law, the

Industrial Revolution, with its radically new methods of power-driven production and distribution, created an urgent need for altogether new and independent fields of law. Activist judges eagerly responded with fundamental changes to English Law, much to Blackstone's dismay and that of his followers.

Blackstone's *Commentaries* notwithstanding, the second half of the 18th century was a period of unbridled judicial activism in England. A host of new and far-reaching commercial and other laws came from the bench concerning, among other issues, negotiable instruments, the sale of goods, insurance, secured transactions, and corporations.

Not only did English Law enjoy a great upsurge in prestige, thanks in large measure to Blackstone, so did the reputation of the English lawyer, whose persona improved significantly by the end of the 18th century from that of a tradesman to a more professional status.

As might be expected, the amount of English Law that spilled over to the colonies in pre-Revolutionary America could hardly be called a legal system. While colonists carved communities out of the wilderness, much of colonial law might best be described as little more than frontier justice.

It took a long time before a system of real courts or a professional class of judges and lawyers emerged in America. In the meantime, English Law was all that American lawyers and judges knew.

After the Revolutionary War, the American Constitution provided an historic opportunity to build from scratch this new nation's governmental institutions. Key to the Constitution was the establishment of three independent branches of government: the Executive, Legislative and Judicial, along with a framework for a system of law for the new republic and its federated states.

Included in the new American Constitution were specific references to Common Law, trial by jury, and the courts of law and equity.

AMERICAN CIVIL LAW

Legal historians have marveled at the deliberate way America's legal pioneers went about structuring the new nation's justice system.

As the conquest of the American continent moved farther and farther west and the country's population centers multiplied, grew and prospered, American Law took on a distinctive shape of its own.

Creating a system of criminal law in America was a piece of cake compared to civil law.

In the criminal code, the law spelled out exactly what you could and couldn't do. For example, the criminal code included statutes that said you couldn't murder someone or steal anything, and if you did, the penalties specified for violations were thus and such.

Civil law, on the other hand, was far less cut and dried.

Unlike the adversarial criminal justice system, civil law was intended to be just that—civil. The goal was to encourage disputing parties to resolve disagreements peacefully and out of court through a negotiating process that eventually evolved into the theory of "Contract Accountability."

Of particular concern to the Founding Fathers was setting standards for a free society and embedding them in the Constitution. Being a republic, they decided that "The People" should select representatives to set the rules and enforce the law.

Despite inevitable battles over legal ideology, a remarkably consistent message in American Law emerged. The goal of American Law, above all else, was to defend reasonable conduct and permit citizens to make free and reasonable choices. Of paramount importance were the laws and rules that guaranteed the individual rights sanctified in the newly-adopted Constitution.

Having undergone 175 years of English domination, our new nation desired a shield of justice that would encourage and protect American individualism. The signers of the Constitution believed that real freedom could only result from people working together to solve problems without relying on government to do it for them. To accomplish that, the concept of shared responsibility, based on fair and reasonable laws, was placed at the core of American jurisprudence.

To kick-start our fledgling justice system, we adopted England's reliance on a neutral judge and a jury of peers to decide disputes based on common law. Whenever English Law conflicted with the needs of the New World, however, it was zealously excluded from our common law.

America also parted company with England on the use of barristers and solicitors to conduct courtroom arguments and handle administrative chores separately. Instead, we favored the more efficient use of lawyers that would perform both functions.

The quality of legal representation in America came slowly, due primarily to a shortage of law schools. Law schools didn't begin to emerge in America until the end of the 18th century. In the meantime, the only requirements to practice law in many of the Western states at the time were that a lawyer needed to be at least 21 years old and a natural born citizen.

The idea that people are free to bind themselves and are accountable for their actions became a key element of American Contract Law, which became the first body of American Civil

Law. The first book on American Contract Law was published in 1844.

In those days, justice meant determining responsibility based on written law or a contract. Unlike English Law, our version of Contract Law imposed liability on anyone who promised to do something and, without excuse, failed to do it, causing a loss to the party owed the obligation.

Initially, American Contract Law was paternalistic, setting limits on contracts that might be unfair to one party or the other.

Early English Law was different. It was based on fair and reasonable behavior. It was also paternalistic, so much so, that for several centuries after the Norman Conquest, English Law did not recognize liability for failure or refusal to perform a promised undertaking.

In those days, according to English Law, a knight could not recover damages from a blacksmith who failed to shoe the knight's horse, as promised, even if the unavailability of that horse caused a loss. The knight could only recover damages in an action called trespass. Under the principle of trespass, if a blacksmith shoed a horse in such a way that the horse became injured, a knight could recover damages.

It was not until later that English courts imposed liability for breach of *any* promissory undertaking. This was called assumpsit. It permitted a knight, for example, to recover damages from a blacksmith for simply failing to shoe a horse, as promised.

Modern legal scholars consider trespass a precursor of a tort and assumpsit a liberalized version of a contract.

What eventually prevailed in American Contract Law is the theory of "Consideration" and "Mutual Assent." These theories guided courts to uphold all contracts, even if by some standards they appeared unfair to one party or the other—as long as they were voluntary. It was the establishment of the concept of accountability, however, that made people free to bind themselves in a contract and be accountable for their actions.

Until the end of the 18th century, there was not a single legal theory for any alleged wrong not covered by contracts. That's when tort liability came into play. Torts became the handmaiden of individual protection. They covered every alleged non-contractual loss, damage or personal injury caused by a defendant.

With the introduction of tort liability, growth in American Law took on a full head of steam.

As the Industrial Revolution took hold in America during the 19th century, it unleashed ample opportunities to explore new legal landscapes in torts, including rights for children and women, as well as labor rights—issues that soon pushed established legal doctrines to the wall.

By the start of the 20th century, the law firmly established a broad spectrum of tort liabilities, with lawyers free to begin applying the concept to a host of ever changing facts and circumstances.

Lawyers took to torts like fish take to water. In those days, lawyers were problem solvers—hired to resolve squabbles, preferably out of court.

Until the 20th century, separation of the legislative and judicial branches of government remained distinct, as the Founding Fathers intended; legislative bodies would make the rules and the courts would enforce them.

Until then, America's reliance on legal precedents and theories as a basis for making judgments was significantly more rigid than in England. That rigidity soon would be tested as the judiciary began adapting the law to society's immense and varied growing pains.

JUDICIAL ACTIVISM

Undaunted by the challenge of changing times, U.S. courts seldom failed to foster the judicial activism needed to adjust America's social and economic landscape whenever opportunities arose. And those opportunities came aplenty in the 20th century.

One of the great proponents of American judicial activism was Justice Oliver Wendell Holmes, known as "The Great Dissenter."

Holmes, long before his appointment to the U.S. Supreme Court, opined in a lecture entitled "The Common Law" that, "The first requirement of a sound body of law is that it should correspond with the actual feeling and demands of the community, whether right or wrong."

Justice Holmes also believed that a society's political majority had the right to press its will on defeated minorities.

What gives life to Holmes' vision of judicial activism is an unwritten system of judicial/legislative checks and balances that works this way:

The U.S. Supreme Court, as asserted by Chief Justice John Marshall, has the power to declare unconstitutional acts of the legislative and executive branches of government, as well as decisions by state courts. The courts, through their decisions, also have the power to create common law and *enforce* it, along with state and federal statutes.

Congress or State legislatures, on the other hand, have the power to enact new statutes designed to skirt constitutionality decisions with which they disagree. Such new statutes also can be challenged on constitutional grounds down the road, giving the courts new opportunities to trump legislative actions with which they may disagree. And so the process goes!

Some might argue that judicial activism, as espoused by Justice Holmes, runs contrary to the judicial attitudes of at least some of the Founding Fathers, who appear more in tune with Blackstone's conservative outlook toward the law.

Consider, for example, what John Adams had to say about the subject late in the 18th century: "The law, in all its vicissitudes of government, fluctuations of the passions or flights of enthusiasm, will preserve a steady, undeviating course; it will not bend to the uncertain wishes, imaginations and wanton tempers of men...."

Notwithstanding Adams' contention, Justice Holmes' opinion that law should mirror popular opinion pales when compared to what the nation actually experienced by way of state and federal judicial activism in the 20th century.

For most of the past 100 years—most notably since Franklin Roosevelt's presidency—the judiciary has repeatedly leapfrogged ahead of society with decisions that in effect "legislated" what the nation's social and economic agenda ought to be regarding burning issues of the time.

Beginning in 1937, for example, the "New Deal" Supreme Court rejected conservative constitutional challenges to federal and state rules aimed at combating the Depression. Moreover, the electoral politics of the mid-20th century virtually guaranteed the continued liberal tendencies of the court, which culminated with the Warren Court in the 1960s.

Under Chief Justice Earl Warren, the U.S. Supreme Court was perhaps the most revolutionary court in American history, according to many legal scholars, including Lucas Powe, Jr., professor of government at the University of Texas at Austin.

In his book, *The Warren Court and American Politics,* Powe discusses the national impact of such significant Warren Court rulings as school desegregation, reapportionment, the elimination of anti-communist domestic security, reform of criminal procedures (the "Miranda" case), school prayer, and pornography.

Thus an important 20th century hallmark of American jurisprudence was the selection of judges for political purposes based not only on judicial qualifications but also on their philosophical and ideological bent.

What became known as "stacking the court" has, in no small measure, contributed to America's growing wariness of its justice system and the public's growing sense of powerlessness when confronted by it.

No wonder legal purists dream of a utopian *Rule of Law* based upon universally accepted principles, rules and regulations that are noble, just, reasonable, compassionate and beneficial to the common good.

As early as the 13th century, the philosopher/theologian St. Thomas Aquinas described his dream of the ultimate *Rule of Law* as, "an ordinance of reason for the common good, made by him who has care of the community."

Cicero described it in the simplest of terms, when he said, "The good of the people is the supreme law."

In a utopian society, the common good would always take precedence over parochial interests. Only then, legal purists argue, could we hope to achieve a perfect *Rule of Law*—a judicial system wherein judges never make laws; they simply follow them. In a utopian society, the law would be so perfect that lawyers would no longer be needed to argue it.

Perhaps then—and only then—would an increasingly cynical society stop imagining this courtroom colloquy—and others like it: "You are a cheat!" one lawyer shouted at another. "And you are a liar!" bellowed the opposing lawyer, at which time the

judge interjected, "Now that both attorneys have identified themselves for the record, let's get on with the case."

LITIGATION MOVEMENT

By the mid 20th century, certainly by the start of the 1960s,
some of the law's once-hallowed rules and ideals began being
questioned, tested and challenged. American Law was moving
inexorably and with increasing speed toward the idea that law, as
Justice Holmes suggested, should be "a servant to the will of
man..." and... "correspond with the actual feelings and demands
of the community, *whether right or wrong* (emphasis is author's)."

The scary philosophy that popular opinion should rule,
morality notwithstanding, flies full in the face of the Founding
Fathers' overriding desire to protect individual rights and the
rights of all minorities against the oppressive will of the majority.
Nonetheless, the upheaval in America's legal ideals continues to
gain momentum to this day.

An important part of the impetus in civil law toward protecting the individual even at the expense of the community comes
from the belief that the more assertion of rights (meaning lawsuits) there is in our courts, the more perfect society will become.

The logic behind the idea that the judicial road to heaven on
earth is paved with lawsuits boggles the mind. Be that as it may,
many of those responsible for shaping our legal system for the
past 50 years or more believed fervently in the assertion of rights
philosophy. They pursued it with vigor, so much so that the number of civil lawsuits filed in America has skyrocketed to about 20-
million a year.

America's pro-litigation movement began slowly and stealthily for some years before picking up steam during the Vietnam era.

Legal commentators, who once denounced litigation as anything but a last resort for solving disputes, began changing their tune. Instead of being reviled, litigation became increasingly viewed as a vehicle for social reform, a way for the powerless in society to assert their rights.

Law review articles chimed in, suggesting that litigation was a good thing and should be encouraged. With more points of legal reference, went the thinking of crusading jurists in the 1960s, law would become clearer and more helpful in guiding our nation.

A pity no one chimed in with the old saying, "Beware of what you wish for because you just might get it." And get it, we did.

It didn't take long before more aggressive and opportunistic trial attorneys came out of the closet and began pressing for removal of the barriers to litigation. So effective was the trial lawyers' campaign (some might call it a crusade) that in less than 10 years—on June 27, 1977, to be precise—the death knell for the stigma against "going to court" tolled loud and clear across the country. On that day, the U.S. Supreme Court, under Chief Justice Warren Burger, erased the *evil* label from lawsuits by giving attorneys the right to advertise for litigants, albeit within certain guidelines.

Until then, advertising as a lawyer was a no-no. Ethical attorneys were supposed to wait for clients to seek them out—not the other way around.

What prompted the Burger Court's momentous decision was an attempt by an Arizona law firm, Bates and O'Steen, to advertise a legal clinic with "reasonable" fees charged for various legal services. Despite disciplinary action by the Arizona Bar for violating Rules against such advertising, Bates and O'Steen fought for the right to promote the availability of their services all the way to the highest court in the land—and won.

The *Bates v. State Bar of Arizona* decision stood in stark contrast to hundreds of years of legal opposition to lawsuits and/or Law as a business.

The Court's decision notwithstanding, state Bar associations continued trying to hold the line against promotional advertising without much success. Some attempted to control advertising by limiting it to newspapers and magazines. Others tried forbidding lawyers from publicizing and dramatizing tragic events aimed at pulling the heartstrings of an increasingly litigation-prone public.

In the end, nothing stopped the powerful pressure from trial attorneys for the removal of barriers to litigation. Eventually, some of the more aggressive lawyers began setting the rules themselves.

Even "ambulance chasing," once punishable by disbarment if not jail, eventually devolved into a right we now see blatantly and ignominiously practiced whenever disaster strikes.

It didn't take long before legal advertising began resembling business solicitations rather than get-acquainted notices. Display ads with headline screamers began appearing with disconcerting regularity: "Injured at work?" "Been in a car accident?" and "Have work-related headaches or illness?"

Ads began hawking a broad range of services, much like a plumber or an electrician: "Experienced and aggressive trial attorneys." Others identified past success records: "$400,000+—Wrongful Death/Medical Malpractice settlement." Some lured potential litigants with implied results: "Get the MAXIMUM settlement." Still others promoted a "no-risk" feature: "We ONLY get paid if YOU collect!"

Not content with being limited to general advertising, lawyers began *targeting* potential plaintiffs and promoting specific types of lawsuits. Soon television, print and Internet ads listed the names of specific target companies and their evil products.

"Ever worked with asbestos?"

"Do you use the Dalkon Shield?"

"Call to see if you are eligible for a cash settlement."

The Supreme Court's 1977 action took a giant step toward erasing any remaining "thou shalt not sue" sentiment from the tort system. In so doing, the court opened the floodgates to a tidal wave of litigation that has been swamping the courts ever since, earning America the unenviable reputation as the most lawsuit-happy society on the planet.

Not satisfied with allowing lawyers to instigate lawsuits and advertise for plaintiffs, the courts acted to make litigation even more attractive by introducing the concept of joint and several liability. Prior to joint and several liability, if a plaintiff contributed negligently to the injury in any way, the plaintiff could recover nothing.

Joint and several liability put another arrow in the litigators' already potent quiver by enabling plaintiff attorneys to appor-tion damages among as few or as many potential deep-pocket defendants as they could identify—and to do so regardless of the degree of involvement by any of the defendants.

Initially, according to the theory of joint and several liability, a defendant with deep pockets could be made to pay 100% of the damages awarded even if responsible for only 1% of the negli-gence. The more defendants named in a lawsuit, the greater the chance of winning something if not all of the damages were claimed. Talk about playing litigation poker with a stacked deck!

Happily, the responsibility for apportioning liability eventu-ally began shifting to the courts and juries. Even so, the deck remains heavily stacked against defendants in the new civil justice system, where joint and several liability can still be seen at work in many of today's class action lawsuits.

ROLE OF JUDGES

In their push to litigate, judges almost overnight changed their role from interpreting law to assessing blame. Arguments, not facts, became coin of the realm in the nation's civil courts.

Courtroom rules of procedure gradually faded away.

No longer did lawyers need to present sufficient facts to warrant a trial. Federal Judge Charles Clark (former dean of Yale Law School) made sure of that as early as 1944 when, in the *Dioguardi v. Durning* decision, he announced that plaintiffs no longer had to provide the court with facts "sufficient to constitute a cause of action."

All a lawyer had to do to get a trial was to assert a claim—any claim, frivolous or otherwise—along with some creative theory that may or may not bear on the facts, and judges would greet it with open arms, knowing full well that the impediments of an actual trial would tend to force legal disputes into settlements 90% to 95% of the time.

It would not be unusual, in fact, for judges to entertain off-the-wall claims, believing such issues would further encourage pre-trial settlements.

The saddest truth of all is that while judges *want* lawsuits, they do not want trials. Judges know—and so do attorneys—that trials are very costly. They are costly and take an enormous amount of everybody's time—including that of judges. They also know that juries can be unpredictable and emotion-driven, often awarding insanely high judgments that bear no relationship to the merits of a case.

Knowing the vagaries of the emotion-driven court system and the huge potential for financial exposure, defendants are leveraged into paying settlements that amount to little more than legal extortion.

So perverse has the U.S. tort system become that it now encourages litigation for everything imaginable (and some unimaginable things, as well).

Take, for example, the elderly woman who bought a cup of hot coffee and spilled it on her lap in her grandson's car, while attempting to remove the lid from the styrofoam cup. Do the same thing and perhaps you can look forward to a $2.9 million courtroom judgment (including $2.7 million in punitive damages, later reduced on appeal to $640,000)—much to McDonald's chagrin and dismay and that of every other coffee retailer in America.

What the courts have done is insure individuals against their own irresponsibility and the vagaries of life. According to this new judicial philosophy, if you stub your toe and break it on the curb of a sidewalk, a jury may well determine that you are not responsible for the accident even though you failed to look where you were going. The culprit, no doubt, would be the city; it put the curb where it did and failed to mark it with a big "Watch Out for Curb" sign. Don't laugh. New York City learned about sidewalk liability the hard way, paying $53 million in 2002 for slip-and-slide complaints.

The city, prompted no doubt by a bevy of legal advisers, has since shifted the burden for such claims to property owners, giving anti-lawyer cynics much cause to wonder if the powers that be in New York City are familiar at all with Cicero's idea that "the good of the people is the chief law."

Chapter 2

...Prowling Predators

"When there are too many policemen, there can be no liberty.
When there are too many soldiers, there can be no peace.
When there are too many lawyers, there can be no justice."

— Lin Yutang (1895–1976)
Chinese novelist-philosopher

After 300 years of doing it right, the American system of civil law experienced a sea change in the middle of the 20th century that has been eroding the character of America and Americans ever since.

It began when well-meaning, but misguided judges, decided society could sue itself into nirvana. The U.S. Supreme Court agreed, giving litigators the right to advertise for plaintiffs and opening a high-speed freeway to litigation heaven.

With marketing tools never before available in law, a new breed of aggressive, hard-nosed and money-motivated attorneys began attracting potential litigants in droves. And the litigation frenzy was on.

In less than 50 years, these increasingly powerful litigators transformed the lackluster tort business into more than a $200 billion a year industry. By the end of the 20th century, the litigating public was filing as many as 150 lawsuits every minute of every working day—with the take-home pay for plaintiffs' lawyers approaching $45 billion a year in 2002.

Clearly, without the public's vigorous participation, none of this would be possible. Why then is society so cynical about lawyers, when it has been such a willing co-conspirator in the outrageous abuse of the U.S. tort system?

The public's long-standing ambivalence toward lawyers is amply reflected in the seemingly unending string of tongue-in-cheek questions such as, "What's wrong with lawyer jokes?" To which the reply is, "First of all, lawyers don't think they're funny—and nobody else thinks they're jokes."

Strangely, while the public's perception of the function and value of attorneys has shifted from age to age, its love-hate relationship with attorneys has not. Until the 18th century, for example, lawyers were viewed as no better than tradesmen—like plumbers, if you will.

Not until the 19th century, largely as a result of the Industrial Revolution, did the reputation of lawyers take an upswing. Lawyers came to be seen as wise counselors, even heroes, fighting for the little guy and the rights of man.

In his book, *The Culture of Professionalism,* University of Illinois historian Burton J. Bledstein suggests that lawyers played a prominent role in the birth of professionalism and an increasingly powerful meritocracy in America during the 19th century. A key year for lawyers, according to Bledstein, was 1854, when the "production" of lawyers outpaced that of preachers. Now that's an irony worth noting.

By the early 1900s, the status of lawyers improved another notch. They became viewed increasingly as the law's unofficial gatekeepers, deterring selfishness from dominating America's legal system (an ironic thought, considering what lawyers had in store for law in the 20th century and beyond).

Behind the legal profession's uneasy march toward professionalism during the late 19th and early 20th centuries were the big law firms that all but dominated the legal world when it came to ethical concerns and standards of lawyerly conduct. Their influence, coupled with the Bar's "Model Rules of Professional Conduct," had much to do with molding model attorneys into "gentlemen lawyers" in those days.

The Bar offered a clear message that professionalism led to the successful practice of law. What gave that message sticking-power was an implicit but unmistakable threat: Subscribe to the rules of ethical behavior or face disciplinary action.

So strict were the Bar's ethical rules that they forbade lawyers from stirring up litigation or instigating it in any way; the mere appearance of impropriety was sufficient to dissuade a lawyer from taking a case.

Not only were lawsuits deemed unseemly, so was incivility between lawyers. The big law firms made it clear that incivility would not be tolerated. Incivility was unsuitable for the social and professional status to which lawyers as a group aspired. The big firms also made it known that playing "dirty pool" with fellow lawyers could be bad for one's career.

All of that began changing gradually and subtly in the 1960s, culminating in the mid-1970s, when the Supreme Court opened the door to a lawsuit landslide in the *Bates* case.

By blessing certain legal advertising, the court in effect greased the way for an eager legal community to more aggressively pursue the massive money-making power of litigation—and to do it in partnership with a public whose growing sense of victimization and entitlement was an ideal target for wholesale exploitation.

Out of that decision swarmed a new and powerful breed of lawyer-entrepreneurs who quickly changed the face of the U.S. tort system and raised litigation to a new American art form.

Law was on the verge of becoming a really big business.

PREDATORY LAWYERS

The introduction of "predator-attorneys" into the U.S. tort system signaled the start of a new era in legal history in which civil justice would no longer be civil or just and lawyers would act more like hired guns than legal counselors.

The goal of this relatively small but powerful group of predator-attorneys quite simply is money, anybody's and everybody's. And lots of it. And they became quite skilled at getting it from vulnerable individuals with deep pockets, from small and large businesses, giant corporations, and even entire industries—scruples and ethics notwithstanding.

So adept at extracting money from defendants have predator attorneys become, that one observer was reminded about how cold it was last winter: "It was so cold that I saw a lawyer walking down the street with his hands in his own pockets."

Many of today's civil litigators are more like high-stakes gamblers than attorneys. They live and breathe the credo, "To the victor goes the spoils!" Their tactics (both in and out of the courtroom) can be nothing short of brutal. For more than two decades they wreaked havoc on an already overburdened court system. They terrorize business and industry wherever big bucks can be made—in complaints against asbestos manufacturers, distributors and retailers, tobacco, healthcare, you name it. They do it without fear of penalty or reprisal. One famous litigator is reported to have said about one of the most tempting targets of all, the healthcare industry, that "Suing doctors for profit is just like shootin' fish in a barrel."

What predator-attorneys do, they do remorselessly, sometimes without regard to the merit of their cases or the ultimate harm they cause. Some of the more aggressive ones go so far as to incorporate images of predatory animals—wolves and eagles— into their huckstering, often offering veiled and not-so-veiled promises of get-rich-quick payouts with no financial risk.

What they don't win from emotion-driven judges and juries, they extract in pre-trial settlements that border on legal extortion. The rationale they use goes something like this: Since a lawsuit may cost a defendant, say, $100,000 in non-recoverable defense fees and expenses, why wouldn't it make sense for the defendant to settle the dispute by paying, say, $50,000 now and save the time and added substantial cost of going to court?

Most defendants settle for legal extortion—not because they have a bad case. They settle because mathematics and the laws of probability indicate that it is *cheaper* and *smarter* to do so, particularly since the outcome of court trials with today's emotion-driven juries can be so terribly costly and unpredictable. So, the defendant says, "OK," to the settlement proposal because it makes the most economic sense.

So focused are predator-attorneys on winning money that their mantra might have been written by that ruthless financial wizard in the movie *Wall Street*, who boasts that, "Greed is good. Greed is right. Greed works."

With most of the hundreds of billions of dollars a year extracted from the U.S. tort system going to the lawyers and other costs of litigation, is it any wonder some of the more successful predator-attorneys rank among the richest people in America?

CONTINGENT FEE AND NO LOSER PAYS

What makes the civil justice system so attractive to litigators? For those who believe law is a noble profession, the system was wonderfully designed to protect the "have-nots" of this country against abuses by the more-powerful "haves" of society. And that's good. The civil justice system accomplishes this through the availability of a "contingent fee" payment option and the "no loser pays" principle.

In theory, the contingent fee concept is supposed to provide Americans, regardless of financial circumstances, access to the best lawyers by allowing attorneys to participate in the financial outcome of cases. As such, the system should provide a counterbalance against the power of big business and big money.

Contingent fee plaintiffs are also supposed to be responsible for miscellaneous expenses incurred in a losing lawsuit. In reality, contingent fee attorneys generally ignore enforcement of such payments because to do otherwise would tend to discourage many potential money-making lawsuits.

As envisioned, the contingent fee system should be fairly self-regulating. If a case doesn't have a good chance at succeeding, the theory is that attorneys won't accept the risk—since their up-front time and money are at stake, not the plaintiff's. The assumption is that most attorneys will encourage potential plaintiffs to drop weak claims or settle them for some reasonable amount.

If a contingent fee lawyer believes a case is strong enough, the attorney may agree to work for a percentage of the settlement or judgment, plus reimbursement of all legal expenses paid on

behalf of the plaintiff. The fee can run from 25% to 60% percent
or more, depending on the case.

Contingent fee cases can be very lucrative for attorneys. A
complaint that results in a $4 million judgment can easily trans-
late into $1 million or $2 million for the plaintiff's attorneys,
almost always much more than lawyers would likely make from
the same case on an hourly rate basis.

Win or lose, the plaintiff pays nothing when a contingent fee
is in place. Only the litigator has any financial exposure—hence,
the substantial payout for winning the case.

So potentially rewarding are contingent fee cases that a recent
straw poll of plaintiff's attorneys indicated that the vast majority
of them would not accept a case on any other basis. In other
words, even if the plaintiff has a very strong case—and the money
to pursue it—that plaintiff will have trouble finding a lawyer willing to work for an hourly fee.

Another benefit of the contingent fee feature is that it permits cases to move forward that would otherwise be too big or too
costly to pursue. Tobacco litigation is a good example. So is
asbestos. And there are many others that involve thousands and
tens of thousands, even millions of plaintiffs who individually
would not have been able to pursue their claims.

A second feature that helps provide access to the legal system
for those who might not be able to afford it is the "no loser pays"
principle.

The idea here is that in a legitimate dispute, both sides incur
expenses and costs. And while a judge or jury ultimately decides
the outcome of a lawsuit at trial, the system in general doesn't
penalize the loser for losing. That is considered too harsh a penalty.

Another reason for the "no loser pays" feature is that a "loser
pays" system could be susceptible to abuse by affluent defen-

dants who might threaten to run up high legal fees to scare off less-affluent plaintiffs.

Even a good case might seem too risky if burdened by the added responsibility of having to pay the winner's legal fees. The "no loser pays" system alleviates that risk for the contingent fee attorney and the plaintiff.

The combination of the contingent fee and "no loser pays" features makes the U.S. tort system the most accessible legal system in the world, according to its proponents. What could possibly be wrong with that?

Nothing, except that it doesn't tell the other side of the story.

In practice, like the two faces of the Roman god Janus, the contingent fee and "no loser pays" concepts function both positively *and* negatively in the U.S. tort system.

On the plus side, they provide the "little guy" with incredible access to a legal system that might be unaffordable otherwise. And that's good.

Conversely, these features permit great abuse of the tort system by transforming contingent fee attorneys into *de facto* partners with their clients. They also allow unscrupulous attorneys to drum up litigation for all sorts of complaints with all kinds of plaintiffs—legitimate and otherwise—who, win or lose, have *nothing* at risk in launching a lawsuit.

The fact is America is the only major country in the world to regularly deny legal fees to the winner of a court battle. It is also a fact that English Common Law, French and German Civil Law—even Roman Law—all agree that it is unethical for lawyers to accept contingent fees; not so in America.

Most industrialized countries prohibit lawyers from working for contingent fees because that would give them a built-in financial interest in the outcome of cases, raising the possibility of a conflict of interest with their clients. Nor do most nations utilize the "no loser pays" feature for fear that the absence of financial risk might encourage frivolous lawsuits.

The often-heard argument favoring the American civil system is that it opens the courtroom to the poor, the widow and the orphan. The problem with that argument is that elsewhere in the world, the poor, the widow and the orphan also get heard in court without a built-in conflict of interest because the loser pays the winner's legal costs based on an hourly fee.

In other countries, the promise of recouping legal fees encourages lawyers to take a solid case from poor as well as rich clients with complaints. But not in America!

In our system of civil justice, it doesn't matter how solid a case may be; legal fees and expenses come out of a recovery before the contingent fee, which can amount to a substantial percentage of *total* recovery, usually a third, sometimes more than half. That's why big fortunes can be—and are being—made almost overnight from contingency fee legal work.

Because of the get-rich-quick potential of contingent fee cases—equating sometimes with hourly rates of $1,000 to $7,000 or even $20,000—most lawyers refuse to accept clients on any other basis.

Despite potential for abuse, contingent fee cases represent a major factor in stimulating America's love affair with litigation. The most lucrative examples are class action lawsuits, which can generate hundreds of millions or even billions of dollars in awards and settlements.

When it comes to mass torts, it is not unusual for litigators to walk away with millions of dollars—and, in some recent cases, even billions of dollars as their share of the take. Individual plaintiffs may receive little more than a relative pittance, depending on the size of the plaintiff base, which can easily run into the thousands and even millions of claims in major cases. In one recent class action, the lawyers received an estimated $30 million, while the plaintiffs received $5.80 each.

An explanation of how the contingent fee works in the real world—particularly when it comes to class action lawsuits—might better prepare plaintiffs for their share of judgments and settlements.

When asked to explain the contingent fee concept, one attorney is said to have replied: "If a lawyer doesn't win your suit he gets nothing. If he wins the suit—*you* get nothing." Such is the *fairness* of the U.S. tort system to those it was intended to protect.

So lucrative is the potential for important contingent fee cases that entrepreneurial investors have begun cropping up in a cottage industry that finances lawsuits in exchange for a negotiated share of the damage awards or settlements. "Champerty," as it is officially known, is a criminal offense in England. While operating under a legal cloud, champerty, nonetheless, is believed to be in widespread use in this country.

With access to substantial amounts of money, this new breed of venture capitalist enables lawyers to initiate costly suits that otherwise would be too risky to undertake on their own.

According to the *Wall Street Journal*, one of this country's more prominent lawsuit investors charges as much as 15% a month in interest on outstanding balances advanced on particularly speculative lawsuits. The *Journal* goes on to report that, while American lawyers are prohibited from advancing personal funds to clients, "some local bar associations lately have adopted rules that permit lawyers to steer clients to outside funding sources without violating their professional code of ethics."

And while the courts in some states have clamped down on such funding activities, the practice appears to be tolerated in many jurisdictions. Sadly, the moral here appears to be if you can't fight them, join them!

For a time, most big "old school" law firms refused to join them. Until recently, most wouldn't dream of working for a contingent fee. Instead, they chose to bill their legal services by the hour. This kept things simple and clear for both parties. It also precluded potential conflicts of interest that might arise from having a vested interest in the outcome of a case. That all changed, of course, when the lure of big contingent fees became too much to resist.

GROWING INCIVILITY

Not only has the substance of civil law changed dramatically over the past 50 years, so has the style of law being practiced. It has become increasingly adversarial in nature and disturbingly more in keeping with its criminal counterpart.

As Bill Veeck, the late professional baseball team owner, put it: "Next to the confrontation between two highly trained, finely honed batteries of lawyers, jungle warfare is a stately minuet."

Here's another description of today's civil justice system at work, as reported in *Newsweek* magazine: Two opposing New York law firms argue over a deposition regarding a big commercial lawsuit. Suddenly tempers flare. "Somebody pointed a finger," *Newsweek* reported. "Another grabbed at a piece of paper, and suddenly three grown men in tailored suits were squirming around on the floor, fists flying among the bodies."

Unthinkable behavior? Think again. What about those "big

law firms" that once demanded civility among attorneys? That was then. This is now. What has changed? Money. That's what.

Yesteryear's image of lawyers as wise counselors collided with the growing perception of the modern lawyer as a hard-nosed *advocate* and *entrepreneur* with pit bull tendencies. Not only had the straight-laced image of lawyers faded from memory, so had the memory of lawyers that once upon a time encouraged potential clients to try and resolve disputes before considering lawsuits.

Scruples and ethical standards had also faded away, as more and more big dollar litigation opportunities stepped across the lawyer's threshold.

By the start of the 21st century, a major segment of the once revered noble profession of law had become a cash cow business run by a growing breed of litigator-entrepreneurs.

Civil Law had grown into a sure-thing industry like none other in history, except perhaps the hotel-casino business—the difference being that today's lawyers get much better odds playing *the lawsuit lottery* than playing blackjack or the slot machines.

Not surprisingly, it wasn't long before some of the bigger "old school" law firms that once upon a time had shied away from contingent fees began taking on some of those big dollar cases.

The opportunity to make really big money was just too good to ignore.

Even so, it would be the smaller law firms and sole practitioners that continued to lead the predatory pack, attracting the lion's share of the contingent fee business.

With experience, they quickly learned how to identify the cases they could win—thus minimizing their downside risk, while maximizing the business potential and profitability of contingent fee litigation.

EMBOLDENED LAWYERS

Propelling the urge to sue in the 1970s was the realization that no one was above the law. Challenging the "Powers That Be" became almost a way of life for many during the Vietnam-Watergate Era.

But it was the landmark *United States v. Nixon* case and the scandal-related Richard Nixon resignation as President of the United States that awakened America to the notion that the rich and powerful did not control the law. An even more powerful idea took hold. If the law could take down a President, it could take down *anyone* or *any company*, no matter how big and powerful, if you were damaged by that person or company.

With that realization, lawyers became emboldened. They became fearless in their pursuit of litigation. Civility took a back seat to tactical considerations. Aggressiveness and intimidation became expected behavior. The huge potential market for litigation was sufficient motivation for lawyers to shed their former wise counselor, hero, and statesman-like images for that of a tough-as-nails winner.

Once lawyers argued civil law with civility, like gentlemen. Today they argue it like pit bulls. Civility and honesty have given way to bullying, impropriety and winning-at-all-costs. Winners get noticed—and get the business—not gentlemen. Since contingent fee lawyers don't get paid unless they win a judgment or force a settlement—a win-at-all-costs mentality has overtaken the ranks of civil litigators.

The trend has not gone unnoticed, particularly among important legal ethicists and judges who express shock and concern at the increasingly brutish behavior of today's civil litigators.

Nationally renowned Penn Law School Professor Geoffrey Hazard, Jr. once described the growing incivility within the legal ranks this way: "Depositions today contain as much argument between the lawyers as questioning of the witnesses . . . Motion papers reek of adverbial abuse and recrimination . . . And oral arguments are more about putting down the other lawyer, than getting the merits of the case across to the judge."

Many legalistic slugfests come not from the heat of the moment but rather by intent and design, according to Texas Supreme Court Justice Eugene Cook. Justice Cook once complained that some law firms go to such extremes as conducting in-house courses on "sharp tactics," including classes on intimidation, gratuitous belligerence, cost infliction, witness coaching, information control, and general all-around incivility.

Not all lawyers opt for the "take no prisoners" attitude that pervades today's adversarial practice of civil law.

Some judges and lawyers decry such behavior. For one thing, it fuels public cynicism about the law. For another, it gives rise to an unending stream of caustic jokes about those who practice it.

Some would like to see a lot less of the pit bull mentality among today's civil litigators, even if it means making a bit less money. They, unfortunately, are greatly outnumbered by those who believe that tough-guy tactics add to the intimidation factor they strive to project when going *mano a mano* in a lawsuit.

Most do whatever they have to do—no holds barred and no quarter given—to perpetuate the litigation culture in America and make a lot of money at it. Their goal is to "win, win, win" at all costs, regardless of the ultimate consequences.

ACQUIESCENT BAR

By the 1980s, the role of lawyers and the *Rule of Law* had taken a serious downturn. Lawyers decided what they wanted.

Money was where it was at. And the public sensed the changes taking place.

Even the Bar acknowledged, albeit reluctantly, the changes in American Law and lawyering, so much so that in 1983 it revised its "Model Rules of Professional Conduct," which had discouraged lawsuits.

Among other things, the Bar began watering down language in its rules. Words like "should" and "shall" were replaced with less restrictive language such as "may" and "it is advisable" to do thus and such.

The many examples of recommended behavior that once guided lawyers through a myriad of ethical questions, all but disappeared.

Once unthinkable promotional practices, such as trolling for clients through advertising, gradually became the norm. The new reality was that lawyers had little chance of professional survival amidst the hundreds of thousands of attorneys who competed for litigation business unless they could tell the world what they did. And tell the world they did!

You cannot watch television today, listen to radio, read newspapers or thumb through the Yellow Pages of a telephone directory without being pitched by some personal injury lawyer suggesting that you are entitled to compensation for any and every misfortune that may have come your way. And you can get compensated for that misfortune, they promise, "At no cost to you. Our fee comes out of the settlement!"

Clearly, the norm for the practice of law has changed.

One thing history teaches us about change, however, is that it is almost always a work in progress. Some jurists, for example, have begun thinking that incivility in the legal ranks has gotten way out of hand. "Enough is enough," they now say.

Could it be that the pendulum regarding acceptable professional behavior has begun swinging back toward civility? Perhaps the recent changes in the Arizona Bar's "Model Rules for Professional Conduct," as approved in 2003 by the Arizona State Supreme Court, are an omen.

In a note accompanying a summary of its new rules, the Arizona Bar says it is replacing a reference to previously undefined "zealous" behavior with the phrase, "Lawyers should conduct themselves honorably."

"Regrettably," the note explains, "some lawyers had misinterpreted the term 'zealous' to be justification for rudeness, belligerence and otherwise unprofessional conduct that disparages the profession."

An editorial comment on the Bar's summary of changes offers this additional warning: "Whether all of this is going to bring about a sea change in lawyer attitudes remains to be seen, but it is pretty obvious that the Arizona Supreme Court has seen enough of what used to pass for 'zealous advocacy.'"

From little acorns giant oaks grow! (*We can only hope the adage applies to attorneys as well as trees.*)

Entitlement Mentality

While predator-attorneys undoubtedly are responsible for the lion's share of the nation's monumental litigation problem, they are not wholly to blame for creating America's increasingly dysfunctional civil justice system.

Without excusing their greed, brutish behavior and over-zealous tactics, the truth is that, as unrelentingly self-serving as many of them are, predator-attorneys nonetheless play the role society created for them.

A second terrible truth is that the much-abused U.S. tort system would not be possible without the courts' encouragement and complicity. Nor would it be possible without the public's selfish participation, or the irresponsible judgments and "we'll-teach-them-a-lesson" mentality of runaway juries.

Unquestionably, *the lawsuit lottery* would be dead in the water if America's once self-reliant and responsible citizens had not, for whatever reason, anointed themselves as "victims" with a penchant for filing lawsuits for every misfortune, real or otherwise, that comes along.

The cold-hearted truth is that, while predator-attorneys may stoke the red-hot furnace that drives America's litigation engine, there would be very little to stoke without the fuel provided by the public's growing sense of victimization and entitlement to whatever it wants.

Whether the runaway tort system has had more of an impact on the American public than vice versa is difficult to assess. Suffice it to say that without the public's insatiable appetite for suing one another, there would be no litigation crisis in America. Equally true is the fact that if the U.S. tort system were less predatory and less encouraging to anyone with a gripe and an urge to get rich quick, the public would be far less attracted to litigation as its first choice for resolving disputes.

What matters most is that these realities exist, and because they do, the urge to sue has become an almost intrinsic part of American life, so much so that even those who think they have little reason to worry about lawyers, lawsuits or judges are being forced to take notice.

In today's litigious society, it is almost a certainty that

everyone knows someone who has battled through some legal obstacle. Another almost certainty is that, with 70,000 civil lawsuits filed every day, chances are your turn is coming, if it hasn't already happened.

Why is this so? Why has litigation increased so dramatically in just 50 years? Is it because Americans are injuring each other more than we did two generations ago? Hardly. The root problem, unfortunately for America, lies elsewhere.

A more likely scenario is that, as America grew rich beyond the wildest dreams of our Founding Fathers, the meritocracy that had been "The American Way" for more than 200 years gave way to something else.

It may be that life had become increasingly easy for most Americans. Even as early as 1960, President John Kennedy saw something corrosive happening to the character of America and Americans, when in his Presidential Inaugural Speech he said, "Ask not what your country can do for you. Ask what you can do for your country."

So affluent has America become that Americans have come to believe increasingly that every problem can be solved with money. Ignored is the real tragedy of modern America. As it has grown rich and richer, our country has become more and more removed from the ethos of personal responsibility and accountability that made America strong, powerful and respected.

SOCIETY OF VICTIMS

No longer self-reliant, Americans have begun seeing themselves as victims of every mishap and misfortune that comes their way. They have come to believe that they can sue for every right they think they have.

Forgotten or ignored is the fact that with every right—every freedom, if you will—comes a corresponding responsibility, and that the two are inseparable.

Americans have come to believe that nothing is their fault; that someone else is always to blame. They also have a growing sense of entitlement to compensation from anyone and everyone or any entity or entities that may have contributed in any way, direct or otherwise, to any injury, real or not, regardless of personal fault.

Seizing on society's growing sense of victimization and entitlement, predator-attorneys helped convince much of the public that it has a "right" to sue neighbors, friends, even family members and employers, doctors, businesses and industries for whatever "wrongs" may occur.

Through advertising, media hype and the actions of lawyers and courts, much of society has been convinced that victimization and entitlement are normal, acceptable forms of behavior.

Accordingly, we have been taught that harsh, aggressive, and vengeful pursuit of cash compensation for real or imagined "wrongs" is the new "American Way." And it is as American as baseball and apple pie.

Worse yet, when victimization is rewarded, it becomes legitimized and reinforced in ways that ultimately are destructive to the so-called "victims" and to society as a whole.

Fifty years ago, most of our parents or grandparents wouldn't know how to find a lawyer let alone engage one. You just didn't sue anyone. It wasn't done. If you got injured, insurance would cover the claim or the offending party would pay the cost of the injury if you were lucky. Everyone involved chalked up such experiences to the school of hard knocks and went on with their lives.

We used to think, accidents happen! No one thought about punitive damages or compensation for trauma, mental anguish, or emotional distress. No one even knew what those terms meant. Not so today.

Confronted by the overwhelming litigation that surrounds us all, and the distrust and disdain society feels toward the law and lawyers, it is no wonder that 83% of Americans surveyed in a recent Harris Poll said they feel "more threatened by the justice system than protected by it."

Even more revealing of the public's negative attitude toward lawyers is the Gallup poll that ranked lawyers next to last in honesty and ethics—just a hair above used car dealers. My, how far the mighty have fallen!

Despite these deep-felt negative apprehensions about the law and lawyers, an American Bar Association survey of its members incongruously indicates that 80% of the respondents think that, "In spite of its problems, the American justice system is still the best in the world." Now that's denial.

"Of course, these poll results were reported by the news media, so they could be wrong," says Dave Barry, the popular American satirist. "There might not actually have been any polls; it's possible that some reporter just made the whole thing up. But I don't think so."

Despite such broad-based and growing public distrust of the civil justice system and disdain for lawyers, the public nonetheless is undeterred in its headlong rush to get whatever can be gotten from *the lawsuit lottery* before it gets them.

No longer does the "Golden Rule" seem to provide the moral compass that once guided so many generations of Americans. That rule seems to have been replaced by a somewhat brassier version of the adage, namely: "Do unto others about 30 seconds before they do it to you. Then split."

In today's "none for all and all for one" society, no one is excluded from the litigation game. Everyone is a player—like it or not. Nor is anyone safe from its potentially devastating economic and emotional consequences. Not me. Not you. Not anyone. Not any company or industry. Not the country.

Some would argue that the American justice system, as originally intended, no longer prevails. So unreliable and devalued has the *Rule of Law* become that the late legal scholar and Yale Law School Professor Grant Gilmore once described it as "a meaningless slogan."

Others would suggest that the fabric of our nation is being torn apart by a litigation rampage that attacks all in its sight, taking no prisoners and replacing optimism with fear.

Perhaps that is why there is so much cynicism about the law and lawyers.

Perhaps there is something innate that causes people to be uneasy and fearful of those who—like some lawyers and judges—can so easily flip their power switch from "help" to "harm."

Perhaps it goes even deeper than that.

Perhaps we have come to believe and fear the one consistent lesson that history teaches every generation, namely that power *can* and *does* corrupt, and that absolute power corrupts absolutely.

Perhaps *that* is the one constant that conditions people's attitudes about the law in general and lawyers in particular.

Perhaps deep down the public secretly fears that the *Shield of Justice* that once promised protection for all has been forged into a mighty sword that now threatens the unprotected.

Perhaps the explanation for America's persistent cynicism

about lawyers is as simple as the image conveyed in Mario Puzo's book, *The Godfather:* "A lawyer with his briefcase can steal more than a hundred men with guns."

Chapter 3

... New National Pastime

"The Bible says somewhere that we are desperately selfish. I think we would have discovered that fact without the Bible."

—Abraham Lincoln (1809–1865)
Sixteenth President of the United States

America is a country under siege. Its economic infrastructure is being undermined; its national character threatened; its legitimacy questioned. Every year, the nation's once-proud commitment to self-reliance and personal responsibility gets whittled away in U.S. courts.

Today, everyone with a gripe wants someone to pay for it, regardless of who's at fault. And they usually get what they want in a civil justice system that over the past 50 years has grown increasingly blind to the injustice and incivility that now permeates it.

The only *Rule of Law* in today's civil justice system is that there is no rule anymore—at least none the public can rely upon.

That's because "suing for dollars" has become big business in the U.S. tort system.

To describe the litigation craze as a gigantic get-rich-quick game wouldn't be a stretch. It's a game being played 20-million times a year in courtrooms across the country. What's the big inducement? A payout bigger than all the legitimate state and national lotteries combined—almost a *trillion* dollars in the past five years alone!

Like it or not, everybody can play the litigation game. And what a game it is. It's called *the lawsuit lottery*. And it has become America's newest national pastime.

Name another sport that gets played tens of thousands of times a day—for *big* money (perhaps yours) with little or no financial risk to plaintiffs who are heavily favored to win a piece of the near-billion-dollar-a-day payout.

It's not a pretty game, but for that kind of money, who needs pretty? Just ask the cynic how it's played, and you're likely to hear the following scenario:

All you need is a gripe and an attorney. You can find them on TV and in the Yellow Pages. You can't miss their ads; they have wolves and eagles and other predatory mascots glaring at you. Or just sit by the phone; one of them may call you, now that "ambulance chasing" is no longer disreputable.

Next, you and your attorney pick a target—someone, anyone and everyone with deep pockets and money in them—who may have contributed to your mishap. Forget that you may have caused it yourself. That usually doesn't matter. Not in today's civil justice system.

Then watch your lawyer sue the heck out of whoever has gotten in your litigation crosshairs. Chances are you'll never go to court. Chances are even better that the threat of an expensive lawsuit will force a settlement, regardless of fault. That's the beauty of today's tort system.

So what if the settlement looks like a shakedown? Legal extortion is OK in today's civil justice system. Just take what you get and run like a thief.

Of course, a big chunk of the money will stick to your attorney's fingers. It always does. But that's OK, too. Heck, you didn't have anything to start with except a gripe and some prey to pin it on! Besides, your lawyer was footing the bill in exchange for a piece of the action—a big piece.

That's how *the lawsuit lottery*—also known as the U.S. tort system—works today, more or less.

As for those not yet targeted to play suing for dollars, maybe they've been lucky. Or maybe their pockets are not yet deep enough to be of interest. Which brings to mind the old adage, "Without money, you need not fear a crowd of lawyers anymore than a crowd of pickpockets."

Could this be why some of the most frequently tort-targeted Americans, especially physicians, are turning increasingly to self-insurance and asset protection to help eliminate the incentive to sue? Could be. But more about that later in this commentary.

LAWSUIT 'UTOPIA'

No other legal system in the world functions remotely like the U.S. tort system. Unlike any other country in the world, America *encourages* lawsuits. The more the merrier, according to many modern-day American jurists.

The intent, or so the rationalization goes, is to sue ourselves into a better world. We can do this, they say, by punishing anyone and everyone that may have had a hand, directly or indirectly, in any mishap, causing injury or some other wrong to someone else—even if the injured party contributed to the wrongdoing.

Those who encourage litigation theorize that the fear of being sued will deter civil wrongdoing and lead us into judicial nirvana. Ignored is the fact that fear of punishment hasn't been much of a deterrent in our *criminal* justice system, which currently houses a worldwide record of more than two million men and women in its jails and prisons. Not incidentally, America also holds the record for incarcerating a higher percentage of its citizens than any other country in the world.

There is another theory about the ultimate objective of today's litigation craze that appears to have a lot of credence. That theory goes like this: Where there is litigation, there is money to be made.

What's more, litigation is an equal opportunity enterprise.

You can litigate money from family members, friends, neighbors, doctors, hospitals, business owners, manufacturers, bankers, and stockbrokers, even government. Take your pick. There is no scarcity of potential defendants primed to play *the lawsuit lottery*.

As British novelist Charles Dickens pointed out in *Bleak House*, "The one great principle of the English law is to make business for itself."

American attorneys have taken the Dickens principle to heart, beyond anything Dickens may have had in mind regarding England's barristers.

Today, America has more lawyers, more courts, and more lawsuits by far than any other country in the world—and the numbers grow with each passing year. The cost of civil justice in America is expected to approach *$300 billion a year* by 2005. That's 100 times more than litigation cost the economy 50 years ago, when the business of lawyering first began to sniff out the huge potential business of lawsuits.

Incredible as it may be, the litigation war in America appears to have cost about *twice as much* in 2003 than America spent its first year fighting the war in Iraq.

While much has been written about the world's most litigious society, the editorial focus generally has been on high-profile corporate negligence and medical malpractice litigation—the more sensational, big-dollar lawsuits that force giant companies into bankruptcy, put tens of thousands out of work, and drive doctors out of medicine. None of this seems to have put a crimp in corporate malfeasance or the marketing of unsafe products, if the scandalous revelations that pop up, with disturbing regularity, are any indication.

Nor has the soaring number of medical malpractice claims tended to improve the amount, quality or cost of healthcare in America. Just the opposite seems to have happened. The amount and quality of healthcare have all declined in the face of rising medical malpractice claims and costs, despite the indisputable fact that plaintiffs fail to prove negligence in four out of five malpractice suits. But that's a tale for another chapter in this commentary as well!

Meanwhile, the increasingly powerful trial attorneys get rich and richer by driving the litigation bandwagon to record highs year after year.

While big-dollar class action lawsuits account for most of the headlines, the harsh reality is that the vast majority of civil lawsuits target Middle America—those small business owners with deep pockets and other middle income Americans, usually those with less than $1 million in vulnerable assets. It's so easy to sue them.

Not so in the past!

It used to be that the U.S. tort system was a judicial forum where legitimately injured people could seek redress. The system has since been transformed into something more closely resembling a game show, where selfish opportunists can get rich quick with little more to justify their claims of entitlement than a capricious gripe and a craving for someone else's money.

Personal injury claims represent the easiest pickings of all in today's civil justice system.

FRIVOLOUS LAWSUITS

While not all claims are outrageous or unfair, many are, especially when an "entitled victim" and a predatory attorney join forces in the dispute.

Many lawsuits are frivolous; and some are downright ridiculous. None, however, can be ignored because all are potential moneymakers to plaintiffs and attorneys alike.

While oddball court cases make for silly headlines and titillating reading, there is no such thing as a laughing matter when it comes to being sued. You can be sued for anything: dog bites, slip-and-fall accidents, broken water pipes, jungle gym mishaps, trespass by a neighbor's tree, or an unleashed dog messing up your lawn! You can be sure that somebody has been sued for just about every conceivable mishap.

Just how off-the-wall can these civil complaints be? Let me count the ways. One that comes immediately to mind concerns the panhandlers who sued Chicago for preventing them from begging on street corners. The panhandlers won nearly $500,000 (of which, $375,000 went to their lawyers).

Then there was the Arizona resident who tripped while trying to outrun an "attacking" goose in a local park and got $10,000 for the fowl deed.

And let us not forget the wisdom tooth extraction that cost a North Carolina dentist $5 million in a malpractice award because, "the defendant used too much pressure and the procedure lasted too long."

Nor should we ignore the woman in Michigan whose landlord told her she could no longer keep a dog in her apartment. She decided to sue instead of looking for a new place to live. A jury awarded her $300,000. Or the Ohio widow who sued a doctor claiming he was to blame for her husband's heart attack. Forget the fact that her husband was overweight, a smoker, got little exercise and ate poorly. A jury awarded this woman $3.5 million.

As for the *really* off-beat lawsuits, nothing is too surreal for America's courts. Take, for instance, the case of a convicted killer who sued New York State for a $650,000 sex-change operation— and a federal judge who allowed the lawsuit to move forward, ordering medical professionals to select an appropriate treatment plan for the prisoner.

No one is immune to this insidious societal disease. No sector of the economy is safe from it. Not even sports. Take football. Earlier this year, an outraged fan sued the Cincinnati Bengals and the National Football League for failing to put a "competitive team" on the field. And what about the high school pitcher who filed a lawsuit against the manufacturer of the baseball bat used to hit a line drive that hit him during a game?

One lawsuit that really defies credulity concerns the California woman who sued her dentist for taking an x-ray that destroyed her "psychic ability" to make a living.

Dubbed "junk litigation," the number of lawsuits industry insiders consider just plain crazy or frivolous are endless. And the incomprehensible awards being extracted by emotion-driven juries boggle the mind. Take, for example, the $175,000 award given by a sympathetic Mississippi jury to the husband who sustained a "broken heart" because his wife had an affair shortly before they were divorced.

Some lawsuits simply don't pass the smell test; they're unreasonable, unfair and ultimately harsh and unjust. Such dubious litigation often involves the theory of "negligent entrustment."

Basically, this legal principle involves providing something potentially dangerous (say, a car or a gun) to someone likely to use it in an unreasonably risky manner. Since the theory of negligent entrustment can be applied to a vast array of circumstances, injury attorneys jump on this theory at every opportunity.

How unreasonable, unfair and unjust can negligent entrustment lawsuits be? Ask the 92-year-old Vermont widow who lost much of her life savings and almost her retirement home because she lent her great-grand nephew some money to buy a car, which he subsequently crashed. The victim's family extracted $950,000 from the widow. It seems she had more money and deeper pockets than her great-grand nephew.

The old woman should have known, the plaintiff's argument went, that her great-grand nephew would likely be reckless with the car and have an accident!

Not unreasonable enough? Then consider the lawsuit against a Texas woman who bought a car for her son to use while he was stationed with the U.S. Marine Corps in North Carolina. You guessed it. There was an accident. Only her son wasn't driving. He let another Marine drive.

Even so, the mother was accused of negligent entrustment and forced to travel all the way from Texas to stand trial in North Carolina. Why? Because she had money; the two Marines didn't. No surprise there.

Unfortunately, the woman's insurance wasn't enough to cover the judgment against her; so she had to pay the difference from her retirement savings.

But for sheer audacity, one must tip the hat to the lawyer who dreamed up the legal theory for a claim by a Florida woman who was gored in her backyard by a runaway bull. It seems the bull escaped from a holding pen, wandered across the highway and onto the woman's property.

After goring the woman, the bull ran off. Unable to identify the bull's owner, the lawyer sued the State of Florida under the *uninsured motor vehicle act*, believe it or not. Don't laugh. It's true. And a sympathetic jury (what else could it be) awarded the woman hundreds of thousands of dollars in damages.

With such lamentable examples of lawyers at work today, is it any wonder they find themselves on the receiving end of such derisive barbs as, "Whatever their other contributions to society may be, lawyers could be an important source of protein?"

CLASS ACTIONS

While the combination of the contingent fee and the "no loser pays" principle made Middle America a ready and easy litigation target for any "victim" with a gripe and an itch for someone else's money, class action lawsuits are where the real money lies in the U.S. tort system.

In general, a class action is a lawsuit where many people with similar complaints join together to sue one person, company or other organization. Some call it the predator-attorney's weapon of mass destruction.

Without a doubt, the biggest contributor to the skyrocketing cost of the U.S. tort system are class-action lawsuits, where lawyers sue major companies for millions or billions of dollars on behalf of hundreds, thousands, tens of thousands, and even millions of plaintiffs who, as the *Wall Street Journal* recently reported, "often don't even know they are being represented."

A growing phenomenon since the latter part of the 20th century, class-action lawsuits have created havoc throughout business and industry, engendering a host of bankruptcies, bringing huge companies and even industries to their knees, and leaving massive unemployment in their wake.

A study by *Class Action Reports* indicates that plaintiffs' attorneys typically chalk up huge fees for these cases—on average, over $1,000 an hour—while their clients often get little or nothing when all is said and done. One auto insurance case cited had the lawyer who filed the suit getting $8 million while the policyholders got $5.50 each, plus an increase on their auto insurance premium.

Arguably the most abusive practice to emerge out of the class-action orgy is the tendency for litigators to "shop" for the most favorable courts in the land, regardless of how tenuous the nexus may be between the defendant, the plaintiffs and the courts.

The most gluttonous havens for torts are in Mississippi, West Virginia, Texas, and Illinois—with Madison County, Illinois, said to have the most tort-friendly courts in America.

As for the enormity of class-action activity, consider that during the period from 1997 to 2000, federal class action lawsuits increased 300%, while state filings increased by more than tenfold.

According to the U.S. Chamber of Commerce, "Abusive and frivolous class action lawsuits brokered by a handful of attorneys are overwhelming the judicial system in certain states."

In one West Virginia trial, about 8,000 people sued 250 companies because of exposure to asbestos. And many of the plaintiffs were not even sick! Strange as it may appear, about two-thirds of asbestos claims now being filed are by the unimpaired. This is absurd!

No longer do plaintiffs have to prove actual damage to be included in such a case. Just being *likely* to get ill is good enough to get a share of the compensation, which—not incidentally—eats into the payment that would otherwise go to actual victims.

So devastating has the impact of class-action lawsuits been on this industry that most asbestos manufacturers have been driven into bankruptcy, leaving mostly peripheral companies to be picked clean by future claimants.

Some of the more familiar names wearing the asbestos-related "Scarlet B" around their necks include Johns-Manville, National Gypsum, Babcock & Wilcox, Pittsburgh Corning, and W.R. Grace. Federal-Mogul's asbestos-related demise was the 15th largest bankruptcy in U.S. history.

Dozens of additional bankruptcies may be on the way, according to *Forbes*. Among the thousand other companies named in suits yet to be resolved are Ford and General Motors. Pfizer has 232,000 claims against it.

Moreover, recent estimates indicate that asbestos-related bankruptcies caused as many as 60,000 jobs to be lost to the economy, plus an additional 128,000 potential new jobs lost due to investments that failed to materialize because of the bankruptcies. Add to that another 8 jobs lost to local economies for every 10 jobs lost as a direct result of asbestos-related bankruptcies. In short, the ultimate potential impact on the nation's unemployment will be huge—and the eventual size of it is anybody's guess.

.   One of the real injustices in today's civil courts is that, unlike criminal law, which protects a defendant against double jeopardy, the deep pockets of defendants in class action lawsuits can be picked repeatedly for the same alleged offense until there is nothing left in those pockets to pick. All that remains is insolvency.

The often huge payouts from batch litigation against major corporations, particularly those related to tobacco and asbestos claims, are the biggest single factor in the explosive rise of tort costs in recent years. The $368 billion "big tobacco" settlement in 1988 alone will provide lawyers, *not plaintiffs*, with about $3 billion in annual fees *for the next 25 years.*

Imagine the size of the war chest this annuity will provide to those aggressive attorneys who are hell-bent on targeting other industries for a taste of the class-action hemlock potion they readily distribute.

The reputed purpose of mass litigation is judicial efficiency. The object is to resolve, in one lawsuit, similar claims by many individuals involving substantially common issues of law or fact.

In theory, class actions make a lot of sense, if the objective is to speed up justice and cut the cost of lawsuits by consolidating hundreds, sometimes thousands, even millions of claims into one giant lawsuit. One problem is that these cases can be very expensive and complex. Another very real problem is that many of these cases concern greed and not justice.

In fact, juries rarely hear class actions, since the vast majority of defendants are manipulated into settling them without a fight. That's because many defendants would rather settle a dispute out of court than risk the millions, hundreds of millions, and sometimes billions of dollars in potential punitive damages that notoriously pro-plaintiff juries have been known to award sympathetic plaintiffs.

Another reason so many cases are settled quietly is that many publicly-owned companies would rather settle that than watch the price of their stock nose-dive from the bad publicity that usually surrounds such cases.

Before a dispute can be treated as a class action, however, the court must certify it as such, based on certain criteria. These include the selection of one individual plaintiff and a set of attorneys that the court must approve to represent all of the claimants in the lawsuit.

Thus, while the organizing attorney may solicit a mass of claimants from all over the country, only the selected "class representative" must appear in the court where that representative is qualified to sue. And that court, almost without question, will be located in the most favorable state or judicial district selected by the plaintiffs' attorneys after they "shop" for the most hospitable venue in the country.

Talk about using loaded dice in a crap game.

TORT-FRIENDLY VENUES

The power to pick a class representative from a nationwide pool of judicial districts gives the class action legal team a significant edge over a targeted defendant. Shopping for the best court forum—regardless of how tenuous the nexus between the plaintiff, defendant and the court may be—is one of the most abusive practices of the current class action orgy. Even so, the lawyer must be careful to file suit in the proper court. That means the court *must* have jurisdiction over the parties involved and the type of case filed.

Although the U.S. Chamber of Commerce describes Mississippi and West Virginia as "toxic breeding grounds for abusive lawsuits," Madison County, Illinois, in fact, is where more class action lawsuits per capita have been filed than any other county in America. Madison County saw a 3,530 percent increase in class action lawsuits from 1998 to 2003. In 1998, there were just three suits and only six years later, a whopping 106 class action suits were filed in the county.

With the number of suits rising from 77 in 2002 to 106 in 2003, Madison County should expect more than 145 class action suits filed by the end of 2004 if this dramatic trend continues.

Madison County also is noteworthy for setting the record for the largest dollar award ever for a class action lawsuit—a $10.1 billion verdict against Philip Morris (subsequently appealed to the Illinois Supreme Court). About $1.8 billion of it went to the plaintiffs' lawyers. The original judge's verdict against the tobacco company over false advertising caused the giant corporation to threaten bankruptcy.

Madison County also holds the record for the largest verdict award to a single plaintiff in the history of asbestos litigation—$50 million, plus $200 million in punitive damages.

For these and other dubious distinctions, Madison County, Illinois, has been variously described as "the jackpot jurisdiction," "tort heaven," and "a plaintiff's paradise."

Why is Madison County so partial to class action lawsuits? In the words of Mississippi trial attorney Richard Scruggs, whose firm may pocket as much as $1.4 billion from his interest in the national tobacco lawsuit settlement: "The cases [in tort havens like Madison County] are not won in the courtroom. They're won on the back roads long before the case goes to trial. Any lawyer fresh out of law school can walk in there and win the case, so it doesn't matter what the evidence or the law is."

In his best-selling novel, *The King of Torts,* Mississippi personal-injury-lawyer-turned-author John Grisham likewise pooh-poohs the importance of trial strategies for class action attorneys.

In his exposé on the inner workings of class action lawsuits, Grisham writes, "These cases seldom went to trial. Courtroom skills were not important. It was all about hustling cases. And making huge fees."

Scruggs and Grisham may well be right in their contention that you don't need evidence to win a big class action payout. Scruggs certainly should know. After all, not one lawyer went to trial or filed an original brief in the national tobacco case, yet those attorneys already have walked away with hundreds of millions of dollars in fees, according to a report by the Manhattan Institute.

Eventually, about 300 lawyers are expected to share as much as $30 billion over the next 25 years, as a result of the $368 billion tobacco mega-settlement. But... then again, perhaps not.

Some states appear to be having second thoughts about paying their attorney's hefty fees. Some already are reneging on deals. Florida, for example, which had agreed to pay its lawyers one-fourth of its share of the tobacco payout, backed away from the deal after realizing it would amount to upwards of *$200 million per attorney.* Florida opted instead to arrive at the eventual legal fees through arbitration.

Similarly, in Massachusetts two law firms that helped win $8.3 billion from the tobacco settlement have gone to court to force that state to pay $1.3 billion in legal fees in addition to $775 million already awarded the attorneys.

Massachusetts refused to pay up, arguing that the amount involved equates to about $17,000 an hour in legal fees, which the state claims violates the rules of reasonableness governing lawyers' fees.

All this dickering about lawyers and money brings to mind the story about an attorney listening at heaven's gate as St. Peter rattled off the lawyer's many sins. "Wait," interrupted the lawyer who was in the throes of defending himself. "I haven't been all bad. I remember giving some money to charity."

After checking his notes, St. Peter said, "You're right. I see that you once gave a dollar to a panhandler and a fifty-cent tip to a shoeshine boy." St. Peter then turned to the angel next to him and said, "Give this guy a buck and a half and tell him to go to hell."

ENCOURAGING MASS TORTS

The class action lawsuit had been used in the U.S. more or less sparingly from 1842 until the 1960s. Its roots date back to the "Bill of Peace" devised by the English Court of Chancery. Initially, English rules were weighted *against* organizing class actions.

At first, the most common use of the class action tactic in England involved shareholders of public companies ganging together with charges of corporate misconduct.

The basis for today's class actions in America's federal and state courts stems from a 1938 Federal Rule, which was amended in 1966 to make it *easier* for lawyers to organize cases involving very large groups of plaintiffs. That's when the big dollar potential of class actions became obvious to more and more aggressive dollar-hungry litigators.

The attraction for class actions became even more overpowering in 1974, when the U.S. Supreme Court erased the rule requiring lawyers to show a significant chance of winning a class action before a court would certify it.

The Court's landmark *Zauderer v. Office of Disciplinary Counsel* ruling in 1985 opened the class action floodgates even more by allowing lawyers to *solicit* injury claims involving virtually any business or other institution. Known as the "Dalkon Shield Ruling," this decision completely blew the lid off the dollar-making potential for class action lawsuits.

The ability of lawyers to troll for clients was further facilitated in 1988 when the court gave them the right to solicit individuals known to have interests in legal services.

By 1989, lawyers were hiring full-time marketing directors and public relations consultants, spending upwards of $100 million a year on advertising—most of it promoting personal injury law.

So wild, wooly and perverse are class action lawsuits that in many cases lawyers sniff out the "wrongdoing" of vulnerable targets long *before* they begin advertising for prospective plaintiffs on radio, TV, in newspapers and on the Internet.

The 1990s brought the Internet into even greater play as an important and cost effective marketing tool for use by more and more law firms to target potential clients. Today, dozens of web pages act as attorney-victim matchmakers, identifying thousands of pending and potential mass torts, citing their targets and allegations, and offering fill-in-the-blank complaints and information on how to sign-up for compensation.

Included in the web page compendiums is information involving asbestos and tobacco, auto and tire makers, silicone implants, the computer and energy industries, dietary supplements, discrimination, fast food, the financial and insurance industries, gun makers, healthcare providers, pharmaceuticals, lead paint, plus thousands of other lawsuits aimed at pummeling American business and industry—along with the names of organizing litigators.

With many of the barriers against outright solicitation lifted by the court and lawyers pumping tens of millions of dollars a year into personal injury advertising and promotion, a veritable avalanche of class actions and other torts is crushing the life out of the nation's civil justice system.

As in typical contingent fee cases, class action lawyers pay the up-front costs and get nothing if they lose the case. If they win, the lawyer or lawyers petition the court for an "appropriate" amount to be deducted from the total award or settlement before distribution to the plaintiffs.

Because class actions are pursued at the lawyer's risk, the potential for exorbitant remuneration is considerable—amounting to hundreds of millions and even billions of dollars in some of the biggest cases to date.

One study estimates that plaintiffs' lawyers in the average class action case earn over $1,000 an hour for legal time expended. That's peanuts according to the Manhattan Institute. According to the Institute, some Florida attorneys in the first tobacco lawsuit will take home a staggering $3.4 billion or about $233 million *per lawyer*. "That amounts to $7,716 an hour—assuming [each attorney] worked 24 hours a day, seven days a week for three and a half years," the report states.

Such hourly rates are chicken feed when compared with the estimated $22,500 an hour being paid out of the tobacco settlement to two law firms by the State of Michigan.

There are also cases where lawyers get almost all of the money, while the plaintiffs get little more than a few bucks and a "thank you."

In a case involving a computer company, the plaintiffs' lawyers got $5.8 million in fees, while each class member received either a $13 rebate on new merchandise or $6 in cash. In another class action case, the lawyers received nearly $2 million from a settlement with a breakfast food company, while the consumers got a coupon for a free box of cereal.

The class action payment that takes the cake, however—that is, until another one comes along—is the case against Chase Manhattan Bank, where the lawyers took home $4 million in fees and the plaintiffs each got a check for 33 cents—but they had to pay 34 cents in postage to claim it!

With the kind of income some lawyers are getting thanks to the U.S. tort system, it is no wonder that the *Forbes* magazine list of America's richest people includes a number of lawyers; several ranked as billionaires.

Asbestos Litigation

Asbestos litigation, the longest-running mass tort in U.S. history, already has cost $54 billion in payouts. It's been nearly 40 years since the first asbestos lawsuit was filed in Beaumont, Texas. Since then, about 600,000 individuals have filed asbestos-related claims against 8,400 defendants.

Estimates are that the number of asbestos complaints could eventually range from 1.1 million to 2.5 million, with an ultimate cost approaching about $275 billion, according to the RAND Institute for Civil Justice.

To date, asbestos lawsuits have bankrupted 67 companies and caused the loss of 60,000 jobs and annual wages totaling $200 million. Another 128,000 future jobs also were lost due to cancelled investments by asbestos defendants. And there is a long way to go before this litigation is finished.

Asbestos may be the best example of how devastatingly costly tort litigation can be to corporate America, individual lives and communities, and to the country as a whole.

Since Mississippi and West Virginia are the only states that allow litigation with very large numbers of claimants, trial lawyers have been shopping madly for friendly venues within those borders. How hectic has the asbestos pace been in those courts? One county in Mississippi (with a population of 9,700) has had 21,000 asbestos cases to consider—so far.

About one-third of all the asbestos complaints filed to date still remain pending in state and federal courts across the country, choking the nation's legal system. Moreover, at least another million claims—perhaps as many as two million—may be filed before litigation ends.

There may be another 1.3-million to 3.1-million asbestos-related claims on the horizon. If so, the economy may lose as many as 423,000 new jobs due to unrealized investment totaling $33 billion.

With most asbestos manufacturers no longer solvent, tort lawyers are targeting even the most tenuous of potential defendants, including those that sold or used only minimal amounts of asbestos in their products, or just transported the material from one place to another.

3M, for example, never made or sold asbestos, but the company was sued nonetheless because it failed to warn customers that 3M masks would not filter out asbestos dust if not used properly. Now that's the kind of way-out complaint that could conceivably spur a cynic to say, "If I had one life to give for my country, it would be a lawyer's."

But there's nothing humorous or simple about mass tort trials, although one might think otherwise, considering that about

75% of the asbestos claims pending in 2001 were filed by the "unimpaired," according to a RAND estimate. That's because, the lawyers explain, asbestos does harm in a particularly insidious way.

They argue that the deadly cancer and other serious health problems brought on by contact with asbestos may arise long after the statute of limitations for such torts has expired.

Thus lawyers have begun seeking huge settlements and getting them for people who are not yet sick—and may never be sick.

Whatever the "un-sick" get from an asbestos jury award or settlement, sadly to say, comes out of whatever would have gone to the truly sick. Now there's modern-day civil justice for you!

The gross inequity of payments to victims and their families from these kinds of lawsuits becomes painfully clear when you compare the $150,000 received by a widow of a shipyard worker who died of asbestos-related cancer with the $25 million awarded by a Mississippi jury to each of six retired railroad workers, none of whom exhibited any form of asbestos-induced disease.

The widow got a little more than one-half of 1% of what each of the railroad workers got; their lawyer argued the railroad workers were "entitled" to such compensation because they *might* get sick.

As might be expected, most asbestos defendants settle out of court rather than risk outrageous punitive damages that an emotionally-charged jury might award. Believe it or not, the defendants opt to settle, often without defending themselves or even, in some cases, verifying claims.

A snapshot of what is gut-level wrong about mass torts can be readily gleaned from John Grisham's *The King of Torts*, in which Grisham depicts the destructive power of greed-driven class actions as "...a scam, a consumer rip-off, a lottery driven by greed that will one day harm all of us."

Now that's the kind of justice system our Founding Fathers definitely did not have in mind when they framed the Constitution.

"Unbridled greed," Grisham says in his book, "will swing the pendulum to the other side. Reforms will take place, and they'll be severe. You boys will be out of business but you won't care because you'll have the money. The people who will be harmed are all the future plaintiffs out there, all the little people who won't be able to sue for bad products because you boys have screwed up the law."

OTHER TORT TARGETS

Having collected billions from tobacco and asbestos settlements, successful mass tort attorneys—eager for new kills—have turned their sights on a host of other big class action targets.

There's no lack of candidates. They just cherry-pick the richest. That's how the class action game is played today. Among those in the current wave of targets under siege are HMOs, pharmaceutical manufacturers, and those who make lead paint, cell phones, guns, and a myriad of other products.

And then there's toxic mold, which appears to be another big money maker for class action attention. The first big mold verdict came in 2001, when a Texas jury awarded a homeowner $32 million. Shortly thereafter, TV personality Ed McMahon sued for $20 million and settled for $7 million.

While mold-related litigation focused initially on warm-weather states, such litigation has since burgeoned into a national feeding frenzy. The largest mold suit to date, for $8 billion, was brought by the resident of an apartment complex in New York City; it was settled for $1.2 million.

The *American Bar Association Journal* thinks so much of mold as a source of mass litigation, it suggests that there ultimately may be more gold in mold for tortsters than in asbestos.

But there may be even bigger money in "fat," if you believe one successful anti-tobacco litigator who is now out to trim America's obesity epidemic. He's John F. Banzhaf III, a professor of public interest law at George Washington University Law School. With 300,000 deaths a year associated with obesity and related illnesses, Professor Banzhaf aims to take the fat out of everything but legal fees, it would seem. In an interview, Banzhaf indicated that, like the tobacco case, it will take some time to lay the legal foundation for an attack against major fast food chains and processed food manufacturers. But lawsuits will be coming, he says.

The first "fat" attack was launched in New York, where a 270-pound malcontent sued McDonald's, Kentucky Fried Chicken, Burger King and Wendy's—four of the world's biggest fast-food chains. He accused all of them of selling high-fat meals that made him obese. His suit didn't go far; a federal judge quickly dismissed what seemed like a fatuous complaint.

That's only round one.

The fight against fat is likely to be a long one—just like tobacco, with all sorts of legal theories being formulated and tried.

Some suggest that a winning "fat strategy" could be similar to that used in the tobacco case—namely, to persuade state attorneys general to begin filing actions against the high-fat food industry to recover some of the public health costs related to obesity.

With the number of deaths attributed to obesity approaching those killed by smoking, public opinion, spurred on by mounting opposition from public health advocates, is already building up a good head of steam against the food companies.

The campaign is sure to get a ton of help from anti-tort reform consumer activists, some of whom are already on record against the nation's fat food purveyors. One reportedly described a Big Mac burger as nothing less than "a weapon of mass destruction."

Meanwhile, some in Congress began preparing a pre-emptive strike against those who would sue fast-food giants for making them overweight.

In supporting proposed legislation, one Congressman said, "It's hard to believe that trial lawyers want to make the claim that 'Ronald McDonald made me do it.'" We'll see.

The way things are going, if class action lawyers have their way, pretty soon there won't be anything we can eat, drink, wear, drive, live in, work or play with or be medicated by. Then what will the tortsters have to spend all their money on?

When contemplating such an eventuality, an old French proverb may seem appropriate to some: "No lawyer will ever go to heaven so long as there is room for more in hell."

Chapter 4

... Tottering Healthcare

*"The most innocent and irreproachable life cannot guard
a lawyer against the hatred of his fellow citizens."*

—John Quincy Adams (1767–1848)
Sixth President of the United States

The ultimate question about the U.S. tort system is not whether it rights wrongs, as intended, and gives everyone access to legal redress. It does that. The more appropriate question is whether the *harm* it causes in its present dysfunctional form far outweighs the good it does.

All the evidence indicates that the U.S. tort system is spiraling out-of-control—that it has deteriorated into a get-rich-quick *lawsuit lottery*, that it is precipitating a redistribution of wealth in America, and that it is deeply eroding our nation's vital infrastructure.

So ominous is the litigation trend that *Forbes* magazine warned that, "If the momentum of litigation costs cannot be slowed, it could easily, in the space of a few years, crush important parts of the economy." The crush is already being felt.

The lawyers' biggest and most crushing victories to date have been in the tobacco and asbestos industries, which catapulted a host of tough-minded contingent fee trial lawyers into millionaires and, in a few cases, billionaires.

One of the nation's most vulnerable litigation targets today is the U.S. healthcare system.

Already tottering from years of wildly uncontrollable operating costs, America's healthcare system is being driven to its knees by unaffordable medical malpractice costs that have caused doctors to quit, hospitals to close, the quality of care to decline, and patients to search for available and affordable treatment.

With the prospect of at least 10,000 medical malpractice torts a year and the continuation of soaring insurance premiums, one can readily imagine the unimaginable—a meltdown of a healthcare system that once was the envy of the world.

As medical care costs escalate out of control, so do the number and size of malpractice claims. It's a vicious cycle, with no end in sight. Increased inflationary costs beget bigger and bigger claims, triggering higher jury judgments and settlements, leading to spiraling insurance premiums, ratcheting up costs to still higher and higher levels.

Spiraling healthcare costs affect everyone. They lead to cutbacks in the availability and quality of healthcare, especially provided by specialists. They reduce public access to insurance coverage and medical services, especially by low-income individuals and rural families.

Unless medical care costs are reined in, the result can only be the further destruction of what was once a pillar of American strength.

An exaggeration? Not by any stretch of the imagination.

Medical Economics magazine says that 40% of physicians had been sued by 1999 and that 25% had been sued more than once. By 2002, the number of physicians sued had climbed to 58%.

"At the rate tort costs are rising," *Forbes* concluded, "wide swaths of the country, particularly rural areas, will soon be without medical specialists [and] …drug companies will elect to stop producing vital but less profitable drugs."

While describing tort lawsuits as "a necessary evil in a market economy," *Forbes* acknowledges the need for a mechanism to make "polluters and incompetent doctors and penny-stock scammers" pay for their misdeeds. "But when the payments lose any tether to the harm caused or the culpability of the defendant, they create economic havoc."

The "havoc" imagined by *Forbes* is becoming increasingly apparent in the healthcare industry, one of the major sectors of the economy tracked by the U.S. Commerce Department's Bureau of Economic Analysis.

At $1.55 trillion in 2002, the annual cost of healthcare in America leaped by 9.3% to about $5,440 per man, woman and child. That's 14.9% of the U.S. economy.

The amount of money we spend on healthcare in America is about *equal* to the gross domestic product of the United Kingdom and France and 50% *more* than Canada's GDP. We spend about four times as much on healthcare as we spend on national defense, twice as much as we pay for education, and about 40% more than we spend for transportation.

Contributing to the spiraling cost of healthcare in America are the costs of malpractice liability. Since 1975, the cost of medical malpractice lawsuits has soared at an average annual rate of 11.9%. That's a growth rate 21% faster than the average cost of all torts combined.

Since 1994, the *average* jury award for medical malpractice has tripled to $3.5 million—three times the average jury award for all torts combined. With *median* jury awards in 2001 exceeding $1 million, a 43% jump in just two years, fear of liability now permeates the entire healthcare industry, drastically altering the availability and quality of medical care in this country.

But it doesn't end there. Like everyone else in America, healthcare professionals are vulnerable to all kinds of lawsuits, not just medical malpractice complaints. They can be and are being sued for discrimination, sexual harassment, slip-and-fall claims and wrongful termination, just to name a few of the more familiar allegations being made in ever increasing numbers.

Many such lawsuits are riding the rising tide of disputes that represent one of the fastest growing areas of litigation today—employment law. As employers, doctors are twice as likely to be hit with a sexual discrimination judgment than one for medical malpractice.

According to *Jury Verdict Research*, 38% of *all* verdicts between 1996 and 2002 involved claims of sexual discrimination. Equally sobering is the report from *Jury Verdict Research* that 67% of sexual discrimination court cases end with the *plaintiff* winning—just the opposite of what happens in medical malpractice cases. This isn't good news for healthcare providers when you consider that in 2000, the mean award for sexual discrimination was a hefty $529,373—which, of course, medical malpractice insurance doesn't cover.

MEDICAL MALPRACTICE COSTS

The total price tag for medical malpractice litigation in 2002 came to a whopping *$25 billion*—more than twice what it was 10 years earlier. That's more than 10% of the total cost of the U.S. tort system—and more than 20 times what it was in 1975.

Paradoxically, most medical malpractice claims result in no payment whatsoever, and relatively few cases actually go to trial. Of those cases that do face a jury, two-thirds end in "wins" for the doctors and hospitals involved.

The American Medical Association takes little comfort in knowing the healthcare community usually comes out on top when it comes to defending themselves in front of a jury.

What worries the AMA is the *growing* trend in the spiraling size of jury verdicts that don't go their way.

Large jury awards for medical malpractice are what the U.S. General Accounting Office believes are principally responsible for driving up malpractice insurance premiums in states such as California, Florida, Minnesota, Mississippi, Nevada, Pennsylvania, and Texas. It is also one of the main reasons why insurers are finding it increasingly difficult to provide essential malpractice coverage.

Most unsettling is the disproportionate influence the trend in escalating verdicts has on out-of-court settlements, where the majority of medical malpractices cases get resolved. Settlements in 1999 cost 30% more than they did the year before.

One of the few astronomical malpractice verdicts cited by the AMA came in 2001. It was for $131.7 million, the largest jury award until then for medical malpractice and more than twice the biggest judgment of a year earlier. Another jury awarded $100 million in a 2001 case involving surgeries and other medical care for an infant born after just 26 weeks of gestation. *Three* of the 10 largest jury verdicts in 2002 were for medical malpractice; they cost between $80 million and $95 million each.

The ultimate tragedy behind the burgeoning cost of medical malpractice lawsuits isn't that medicine is failing the public. It is that the *public* is contributing significantly to the failure of health-care in America.

How does that correlate with doctors and hospitals getting sued 10,000 times a year? Because anyone—any doctor, any hospital—can be sued at any time for any reason, justified or not.

How valid are most of those 10,000 lawsuits? Not very, based on courtroom results and on a study by Harvard researchers.

What the Harvard study found was that negligence is not a factor in four out of five medical malpractice lawsuits. Moreover, physicians *win* the large majority of cases that go to court—62% at last count.

Despite the many weak and bogus lawsuits and overwhelming absence of negligence in patient care, medical malpractice lawsuits nonetheless continue bombarding the healthcare industry, as aggressive entrepreneurial attorneys join with self-styled "victims," acquiescent judges and sympathetic juries to jack up the price of healthcare beyond rationality and affordability.

What should be obvious to all is that no matter who wins a medical malpractice lawsuit, *every* claim is costly not only to the healthcare industry and its insurers, but also to anyone and *everyone* with a healthcare problem, including those who precipitate the crisis.

When it comes to medical malpractice lawsuits, *everybody* gets penalized, one way or another.

We see the adverse ripple effect of malpractice litigation in the growing number of Americans losing access to affordable health-care. There are more than 43 million Americans without health-care insurance. And for every 10% hike in insurance premiums, 3%–4% fewer people choose not to purchase healthcare coverage, according to the *Journal of Health Economics*.

We see more and more doctors, fearful of liability, refusing to perform risky medical procedures, abandoning medical specialties, moving out of tort-friendly states, retiring early and quitting medicine altogether.

We see how the fear of liability results in huge amounts of healthcare resources being squandered by physicians practicing defensive medicine.

We see a growing number of hospitals and clinics shutting down or cutting back on emergency, trauma and other vital medical services because of the inability to retain or recruit doctors in tort-friendly areas of the country.

We see the quality of patient care declining as physicians adjust medical care to minimize the risk of liability and adopt a culture of secrecy, which often results in medical errors that go undetected and uncorrected.

We see how increasingly difficult it is for patients to gain access to affordable quality medical care.

And we see how the "victimized" public—those who believe they should be compensated for every medical misfortune (including acts of God and those no doctor could prevent)—is reshaping a system of medicine that is worse today than yesterday, and will in all probability be worse tomorrow than today unless there is quick and dramatic intervention.

If a Harris Poll of 300 physicians is any indication, malpractice costs already have had a deleterious effect on the practice of medicine in America. According to the poll, three out of four physicians believe the quality of patient care is being adversely affected by fear of liability.

Of those queried: 80% say they order more tests than medically needed; 60% refuse to suggest how to reduce medical error due to fear of liability; 54% know doctors who have hesitated while off-duty to help an injured person because of potential liability; 74% refer patients to specialists more often than previously; 51% recommend invasive procedures more often than necessary; and 41% prescribe more medication and tests than required.

FEAR OF LIABILITY

The National Institute of Medicine confirms that fear of liability is adding to the runaway cost of healthcare. The *Quarterly Journal of Economics* places the cost of defensive medicine at about $50 billion a year.

The AMA warns that the prevailing adverse legal climate, coupled with the soaring cost of malpractice insurance, is prompting increasing numbers of physicians to walk away from higher-risk specialties or retire early, leaving patients in the lurch to hunt for alternative providers.

A recent study of hundreds of physicians (age 50 to 65) by a leading recruiting firm indicates that within the next three to five years, 8% of the physicians surveyed will retire, 20% will withdraw from patient-care activities, and 23% will reduce their workloads in one fashion or another. Importantly, 50% said they would not choose medicine as a career.

In another research study—this one an American Medical Association survey of would-be doctors—40% of the 4,000 medical school students interviewed said they would avoid practicing in the malpractice crisis states identified by the AMA. Forty-eight percent indicated fear of liability would affect whether they choose to practice a high-risk specialty.

Included among the 19 crisis states recently identified by the AMA as suffering from the highest percentage increases in insurance premiums are: Arkansas, Connecticut, Florida, Georgia, Illinois, Kentucky, Mississippi, Missouri, Nevada, New Jersey, New York, North Carolina, Ohio, Oregon, Pennsylvania, Texas, Washington, West Virginia, and Wyoming. In addition, the AMA identified nine other states with malpractice insurance problems.

Obstetrics and other high-risk specialties tend to be the most tempting targets for medical malpractice lawsuits and the most susceptible to emotion-driven jury verdicts.

When asked why there is a deluge of lawsuits aimed at them, physicians will likely say that it's because Americans have been conditioned into believing they are "entitled" to a perfect outcome in medicine—every time. But nothing in medicine is perfect, they explain. There is always risk. And risk is a big reason why the cost of malpractice insurance (especially for high-risk specialists) has been driven to prohibitive heights.

How costly is malpractice insurance? From 1975 to 2000, medical malpractice insurance premiums in the U.S. jumped five fold! In Washington State, a full-time family physician *not* engaged in obstetrics or surgery pays $9,768 a year or about *one-fourth* the $37,449 premium paid by a doctor who also delivers babies. Meanwhile, the annual premium for a *full-time* obstetrician runs almost 40% higher—as much as $51,878 for a policy with a mere $1 million limit. That's in Washington.

Premiums in Washington can be a lot different than elsewhere in the country. A small hospital in the rural Arizona border town of Bisbee, for instance, had to close its maternity ward because the hospital's obstetricians couldn't afford $88,000 a year in insurance premiums. (Since then, several women have had babies delivered while en route to the nearest hospital—60 miles away.)

But that's not the worst of it. If an obstetrician is hit with a malpractice lawsuit after a difficult delivery of a baby with, say, cerebral palsy, juries have been known to award verdicts involving tens of millions of dollars to cover a lifetime of care—*even though delivering doctors are almost never at fault.* One case resulted in a jury award of $111.7 million to a child born with permanent brain damage.

Is it any wonder more and more obstetricians and other high-risk specialists are moving to less tort-friendly states or changing medical fields?

A study at the University of Nevada medical school concludes that 42% of the obstetricians in southern Nevada planned to move unless the malpractice cost environment changed dramatically. Many did. The area involved includes the city of Las Vegas, which recorded 23,000 births in 2001 and where 76% of obstetricians had been sued at least once and more than half had been sued *three times* or more.

The Las Vegas exodus caused the American College of Obstetricians and Gynecologists to describe southern Nevada as "the worst place in the country for women trying to find prenatal care."

In addition to losing obstetricians, the University of Nevada Medical Center had to shut down the state's top trauma care facilities for 10 days when surgeons walked out over unaffordable insurance premiums.

The UNLV trauma center reopened after the physicians became temporary county employees, which significantly lowered exposure to medical liability awards.

Some obstetricians would rather quit their specialty than pay the price it takes to stay. One Massachusetts physician made the switch from obstetrics to anesthesiology because of a malpractice lawsuit that went on for six years before being dismissed.

In tort-friendly Mississippi, the obstetrician problem got so bad that most cities with populations under 20,000 no longer had doctors willing to deliver babies. In some areas, women had to travel for hours for prenatal care and delivery.

Other high-risk specialists also are being forced to curtail their practices or are being driven out of their specialties altogether.

When neurosurgeons abandoned their practices in West Virginia, stroke and trauma victims had to be helicoptered 70 miles to Pittsburgh for treatment.

In Delaware County—outside Philadelphia—a group of 18 physicians also stopped doing surgery and answering trauma calls.

UPROOTING MEDICAL PRACTICES

A more draconian option for physicians is to uproot their medical practices and move to friendlier tort zones, making it extremely difficult for some patients to find adequate (let alone affordable) medical care.

One doctor opted out of Philadelphia when he got hit with a $50,000 increase in his malpractice insurance premium. He resettled in Georgia, where the premium was just $2,000 more than the $12,000 he had been paying and where there is a lot less fear of lawsuits.

Many physicians and dentists in Mississippi, beset by unrelenting lawsuits, unconscionable jury verdicts and declining availability of malpractice insurance, created a political firestorm recently by threatening to relocate to nearby Louisiana, where the laws limit liability awards.

Some doctors moved out of state, unwilling to wait and see if the State Legislature and the governor would agree to cap awards for non-economic damages in malpractice cases.

Mississippi eventually did just that, but not before some insurers refused to write new policies and others walked away from the claim-ridden market. According to U.S. Department of Health & Human Services, 15 insurers left the Mississippi market in the past five years.

A third option for physicians fearful of malpractice liability is to quit medicine altogether. A shocking 43% of AMA members said they considered doing just that. One of them is a Mississippi neurosurgeon who, after seven years of practicing medicine, came to see his patients as adversaries. He quit medicine for law school.

In recent years, with the cost of claims soaring, medical malpractice insurers have begun withdrawing from some of the more litigious markets and otherwise limiting coverage. Some have gotten out of the business altogether. Others have gone belly up amidst a firestorm of claims.

According to the Insurance Information Institute, the cost of medical malpractice insurance began taking off like a rocket in 2000, "after almost a decade of essentially flat prices." The institute attributes spiraling premium increases mostly to "the growing size of claims, more frequent claims in some urban areas, and soaring defense costs."

Another less talked about but no less pertinent factor prompting insurance premiums to skyrocket was the recent economic recession and steep decline in the stock market. With investment income plummeting, the profit cushion against claims insurers once relied upon quickly dissolved. To help compensate for the enormous profit squeeze, insurers jacked up the price of insurance well beyond what market conditions warranted.

Insurers Quitting

Faced with soaring claims and disappearing profits, medical malpractice insurers began dropping out of the market, sparking a "crisis of availability" similar to that experienced 20 and 30 years earlier when the public first began feeling "victimized" by doctors and hospitals. Until then, medical malpractice claims were relatively uncommon.

It wasn't until the start of the 1970s that society's growing sense of victimization and entitlement began seriously impacting the healthcare industry. It began suddenly and grew rapidly.

About 80% of the medical malpractice lawsuits filed during 1930–1975 came in the last five years of that 45-year period. Losses sustained by insurance carriers in those five years caused a rapid contraction in available medical malpractice insurance, just as it has today.

Filling that relatively-short lived void were as many as 100 new specialty insurers established across the country by state medical and hospital associations. Funded by the healthcare providers they insured, these new carriers eventually grew to insure about 60% of the national market.

By the mid-1980s, a second "crisis of affordability" emerged, as malpractice carriers once again faced mounting losses—this time due to the increased number of claims and the escalating size of non-economic damages being awarded to the "victimized" public by increasingly sympathetic juries.

Some carriers left the market then, as they did in the 1970s. Those that remained imposed premium increases of up to 60% in both 1985 and 1986.

Unlike the crises of the past, the current medical malpractice insurance crisis is one of both affordability *and* availability. This is due, in no small measure, to the continued unwillingness of state legislatures and the federal government to enact fundamental tort reform, particularly with regard to capping non-economic damages. (Awards for non-economic claims, such as pain and suffering came to an estimated $55.7 billion or about 24% of total U.S. tort system costs in 2002.)

"Over the past couple of years, a number of insurers have withdrawn from the malpractice market completely," according to the Insurance Information Institute. "Others in poor financial condition have been forced to stop selling policies by state regulators."

So volatile is the current medical malpractice insurance market that the nation's second largest malpractice insurer, St. Paul Insurance, pulled out of the market completely after incurring nearly $1 billion in losses. St. Paul found itself spending almost $2 in malpractice costs for every $1 of premiums received. In one year alone, St. Paul saw the number of $1 million-plus claims double.

In its turbulent wake, St. Paul left 42,000 doctors and 750 hospitals in need of replacement coverage. It is estimated that when existing policies expire, affected doctors may pay as much as 300% more for new coverage.

All across the country, medical malpractice insurers are closing shop, it seems. American Physicians Assurance began pulling out of the Florida market in 2002, leaving 2,200 policyholders searching for new insurers.

In Pennsylvania, one of the malpractice crisis states identified by the AMA, the number of insurers dropped from 10 to 2 in five years. In Washington, four medical malpractice insurers went belly-up in as many years; a fifth insurer went bankrupt there in 2002.

One of the states hardest hit by the exodus of malpractice insurers is tort-friendly Mississippi, which lost 15 insurers in five years, leaving hundreds of doctors scrambling to find necessary coverage.

Physician-owned Medical Insurance Exchange exited Nevada in 2004 after 25 years, following that state's failure to enact tougher liability laws.

In response, the Nevada State Medical Association warned that more doctors will be forced to leave the state or curtail their medical practices if they can't find available and/or affordable insurance.

"The state already has too few doctors," the Association said, "after losing nearly 150 physicians in the past year because of medical liability issues." And there is growing fear that the "crisis of availability" in affordable malpractice insurance may get a lot worse before it gets better.

One 78-year-old Nevada family physician, whose policy with Medical Insurance Exchange terminated after 25 years, said he intends to move to Arizona where there are doctors that can take care of him in his old age. "All the good doctors here will be gone," he quipped.

The Washington State Medical-Education and Research Foundation attributes the growing medical malpractice crisis to the tort system's lottery mentality and the "incentives that promote and inflate claims and suits without merit."

"In some respects," the Foundation suggests in its 2002 report, "society has become desensitized to the 'value' of money, just as it has to violence." The Foundation blames "plaintiff attorneys" for lobbying hard and successfully against tort reform.

"The national tobacco and asbestos litigation in recent years has given (the lawyers' lobby) unprecedented resources with which to fight to preserve the present tort system," the report complains.

PHYSICIANS 'STRIKE' BACK

Fed up with the endless stream of lawsuits and ballooning medical malpractice insurance costs, physicians have begun fighting back economically and politically.

Some physicians are so desperate for cost relief that they have begun recruiting patients from managed care networks by forgoing co-insurance and deductible payments that health plan members otherwise must pay.

These doctors, according to a *New York Times* report, "can afford to pass up the payments because the out-of-network fees they collect from insurers often are higher than those they would collect as members of the health plan's network."

While conceding that physicians should consider waiving co-payments if they pose "a barrier to needed care because of financial hardship," the American Medical Association warns, however, that "routine waivers of co-payments may constitute fraud under state and federal law."

What may prove more effective in the long run are the highly-publicized job actions and political rallies initiated by physician groups across the country early in 2003. The hope is that state and federal officials would step in and do something constructive about liability before the healthcare system comes crashing down.

The physicians' nationwide backlash began in earnest in July 2002, when 50 Las Vegas doctors walked off the job shutting down the city's only trauma center. The walkouts spread to Florida, Mississippi and Pennsylvania.

The so-called job actions also spread to West Virginia, where two dozen surgeons at four West Virginia hospitals temporarily refused to operate on patients.

By February, strikes, slowdowns and rallies had spread throughout the entire state of New Jersey, launching the first and largest statewide physicians' protest in history—as thousands of doctors walked out of hospitals and closed down their offices.

About half of New Jersey's 22,000 physicians are said to have participated in that state's job action "in one form or another," according to the Medical Society of New Jersey. The slowdown lasted several days and involved only non-emergency medical care and services.

The physicians' stated objective was to draw government attention to the problem by forcing the public to visit hospital emergency rooms for routine medical complaints.

Despite the slowdown, physicians continued to provide emergency surgical operations and other critical care procedures, without interruption.

About 700 healthcare workers picketed in Neptune, N.J., outside Jersey Shore Medical Center carrying signs reading, "Having a Medical Emergency? Try calling 1-800-LAWYERS."

Others marched in Woodbridge and Paramus, N.J. More than 1,300 paraded outside the State Capitol in Trenton, hoping to pressure New Jersey Governor James McGreevey and the State Legislature into enacting reforms that would curb rising malpractice premiums and cap "pain and suffering" liability at $250,000.

That was only the beginning of the backlash by doctors against rising medical malpractice costs.

On June 13, 2004, *USA Today* reported that hospital administrators and doctors across the nation have begun "striking back against lawyers with hardball tactics that, in some cases, are raising ethical questions."

According to the *USA Today* news story, "Some doctors are refusing to treat lawyers, their families and their employees, except in emergencies." One doctor was quoted as saying that while the idea of refusing to treat lawyers "may be repulsive," it is justified and necessary. As to whether the notion runs counter to the Hippocratic oath taken by doctors, the Charleston, S.C. surgeon, said, "Physicians are not bound to treat everybody who walks through their door."

The surgeon also said he intended to urge the American Medical Association, which has been silent on the issue, to endorse the tactic at the AMA's forthcoming annual meeting. The chances of that happening are not likely. What is likely is that the AMA will continue to doggedly back federal legislation aimed at capping pain and suffering awards in medical malpractice cases, while local medical societies are doing the same at the state level.

What is also likely is that the nationwide dispute between doctors and lawyers will grow increasingly bitter and, some might say, downright spiteful. Here are just a few examples of the trend as cited in the *USA Today* report.

One Texas medical center recently fired a highly-skilled nurse, despite a nationwide shortage of nursing help, because her husband works for a law firm that litigates medical malpractice cases. The fact that her husband practices in a different field of law made no difference. The hospital, according to the news story, has an unwritten rule of not employing spouses of lawyers who represent plaintiffs in medical malpractice or personal injury lawsuits "because of the perceived likelihood of a conflict of interest."

In New England, a well-known neurosurgeon informed the head of the New Hampshire Trial Attorneys that if he lobbied against limits on malpractice suits, the surgeon would refuse to operate on him should that ever become necessary. The surgeon complained that his malpractice insurance premium exceeded his take home pay by $20,000 a year.

Elsewhere in the country a Texas radiologist attempted to discourage frivolous lawsuits by setting up a national database of patients and lawyers who have sued for malpractice. The site was shut down soon thereafter when some of those listed complained about having difficulty securing needed medical care. *(Don't be surprised if the Internet idea pops up again—this time originating in the Bahamas or some other offshore web page site, where liability is not a problem.)*

Even more disturbing to the legal fraternity, according to the *USA Today* report, "are the efforts to silence doctors from testifying as expert witnesses on behalf of plaintiffs." Several months ago, a Florida hospital went so far as to revise its employee policies so that its staff would be prohibited from testifying for malpractice plaintiffs *but not as witnesses for hospitals and doctors*. Now there's a double standard for you. Meanwhile a Jersey City, N.J., hospital removed its chief of staff because, as *USA Today* reported, "he backed malpractice legislation that many of his colleagues opposed."

Perhaps the best summation of what's going in medicine today was made by an emergency care physician, Dr. Bruce Bonanno, who warned that without tort reform, "The system's going to die." Another physician described the healthcare situation as "a ticking time bomb."

The scariest scenario of all came from the president-elect of the Camden County Medical Society, who said that the New

Jersey physicians who participated in those recent job actions were giving the public a peek into the future of what can be expected unless there is real tort reform.

His meaning was clear. Without tort reform and realistic limitations on malpractice liability, the outlook for healthcare in America is grim and growing grimmer.

Watching the nation's healthcare system bleed to death, a cynic might well be reminded of the difference between a lawyer and a leech. "When you die, a leech stops sucking your blood and drops off."

Chapter 5

... Tortuous 'Taxes'

*"The rule of law can be wiped out in one misguided,
however well-intentioned, generation."*

—Attorney William T. Gossett (1904–1998)
Former President, American Bar Association

On October 19, 1765, a Congress of American colonies met in Philadelphia to petition Britain for repeal of the Stamp Act and other oppressive taxes. In its petition, the colonists wrote, "… it is inseparably essential to the freedom of a people…. that no taxes be imposed on them, but with their own consent…"

The idea that taxation without representation was tyranny rose to a rallying cry that resonated throughout the colonies during the ensuing Revolutionary War.

History has a way of repeating itself. Alarmist talk? Not a bit.

The intent here is to arouse public and government awareness of one of the most pernicious taxes of all—a "tax" that

Americans have been paying for more than 50 years without their knowledge or consent—and to call attention to the destructive effect it is having on the character of America and Americans.

Some call it a "tort tax." And every dollar of it goes to fund the great American *lawsuit lottery*, otherwise known as the U.S. tort system—where anyone with a gripe, meretricious or otherwise, has a chance to get rich quick at someone else's expense.

So well buried is the "tort tax" that the vast majority of Americans hasn't a clue about its existence or the ultimate cost to themselves individually or our nation as a whole.

Even so, you won't find any reference to the tort tax in any Internal Revenue Service bulletin. Nor will you find it mentioned on your individual or business tax return.

It doesn't matter. Nor does it matter that the tort tax is collected in a courtroom as a judgment instead of in a retail store as a tax. What it's called isn't the issue. If something *looks* like a tax and *acts* like a tax, chances are it *is* a tax—in this case, a tort tax.

Whatever you call it, the one irrefutable reality is that every U.S. citizen subsidizes the cost of the U.S. tort system to the tune of hundreds of billions of dollars a year.

Much of the cost is buried in what we pay for just about every product and every service we purchase. Only we don't know it because it's buried in the purchase price.

There is a tort tax hidden in the cost of the cars we drive and the gas that runs them. We pay it when we buy homes or purchase paint for the walls or toys for our children. It's in the cost of travel, the cigarettes we smoke, in the food we eat and the refreshments we drink.

We pay the tax when we purchase the medical services and pharmaceuticals needed to stay healthy and remain alive.

It's built into the cost of insurance we buy to protect ourselves from just about everything and everybody—if only it did, and if only we could afford all of the coverage needed.

Every year the cost per citizen of the tort tax climbs—from $89 in 1950 (adjusted for inflation), to $183 in 1960, to $314 in 1970, $410 in 1980, $716 in 1990, $668 in 2000, up to $809 in 2002, according to the Tillinghast division of Towers Perrin, one of the world's leading actuarial consultants.

"Absent sweeping structural changes to the U.S. tort system," Tillinghast estimates, "annual increases will be in the 6% to 11% range for the next several years. At this rate of increase, the burden of tort costs could approach $1,003 per U.S. citizen by 2005."

Imagine the reaction from America's citizenry when it realizes that the cost of their litigious society is equivalent to about a 5% across-the-board tax on wages—*and that the public has absolutely nothing to say about it!*

One can only imagine how the Minutemen who ignited the rebellion against Britain more than 225 years ago might react to being saddled with such an onerous tax without the people's knowledge or consent.

Since 1950 (the earliest year for which comprehensive tort costs are available), the American people have paid an aggregate of about *$3.3 trillion* for the privilege of suing each other.

Growing three times faster than the nation's economy as a whole, the nation's tort tax will have increased 140-fold since then, from $1.8 billion in 1950 to a projected $253.2 billion in 2003.

Time and again, the tort tax has proven its tenacity and propensity for growth despite wide fluctuations in the U.S. economy. Even amidst the nation's most recent economic recession, the tort tax muscled its way onward and upward into the 21st century with a 6.3% gain in 2000, a whopping 14.3% increase in 2001, and another 13.3% jump in 2002.

If Tillinghast's projections prove accurate, the tort tax may leap to as much as $298.1 billion in 2005 or about 2.45% of that year's anticipated gross domestic product.

Viewed in a global context, the estimated cost of the U.S. tort system in 2002—at $233.4 billion—was (based on purchasing power parity) about the size of the *combined* economic output of Denmark and New Zealand and more than twice the size of Ireland's gross domestic product!

Assuming, as Tillinghast does, that the public's unquenchable thirst for litigation continues expanding at a compound annual rate of 9.8% (as it has for the past 50 years), another *$3 trillion to $4 trilllion* will be paid out to society's self-proclaimed "victims" and their lawyers during the next decade. That's more than the cost of the U.S. tort system for the previous half-century!

ALTERNATIVE USES OF TORT TAX

But there are other equally important ways to look at tort costs than as a legalized method for redistributing wealth in America.

For instance, what else could the public spend a couple of hundred billion dollars a year on besides filling the coffers of a growing army of entrepreneurial attorneys and their self-anointed victims?

Surely some of the trillions of dollars in tort costs expected over the next 10 years could be used to find a cure for cancer? *(About 1.3-million Americans are expected to develop cancer this year; more than a half million will die from it.)*

What about a cure for multiple sclerosis? (*MS currently afflicts about 2.5 million people worldwide, including 400,000 Americans.*)

Or AIDS? (*Of the 1-million Americans carrying the deadly HIV/AIDS virus in 2002, half are not now receiving care. As many as 42 million have the disease worldwide, most without much access to any care or treatment whatsoever.*)

And what about the myriad other grave illnesses and debilitating diseases afflicting the world today?

There are the homeless in America and elsewhere, for instance, many of whom are experiencing mental illness. What about them? (*As many as 3.5-million Americans experienced homelessness in 2003.*)

And what about the less fortunate in other countries? (*The U.S. foreign aid for 2002 was $12.9 billion, but even so, as a percentage of GNP, it is the lowest of any industrialized nation.*)

While thinking about helping needy people elsewhere in the world, let's not ignore world hunger. (*There are 1.2 billion poor people in developing countries who live on less than $1 a day; about 850-million people go to bed hungry every night, most of them in the developing world.*)

As startling a statistic as it may be, just 15% of the amount of money spent by Americans on torts every year would be enough to provide adequate food, water, sanitation, basic education and healthcare for every developing country in the world, according to calculations by the United Nations Development Program.

Many of these or other equally worthy activities might have been undertaken without costing Americans a dime more than they already spend on suing each other—if only we had the compassion and the will to do so.

GREED-DRIVEN LITIGATION

Today, greed drives the U.S. tort system—not justice or fairness, and certainly not benevolence. Unremitting greed is what precipitated the litigation meltdown that is destroying everyone and everything in its way.

How greedy does it get?

Consider this: Assuming every civil claim paid in 2003 *deserved* to be paid—and that's an assumption few would make—only 22% of that year's projected tort tax of $253.2 billion or $55.7 billion would be compensation for actual economic loss, e.g., medical expenses, lost wages, etc. Another $60.8 billion would be for so-called "pain and suffering," which can't be measured, but which emotion-driven juries nonetheless dole out by the shovelful to plaintiffs.

The remainder, a whopping $136.7 billion, would go to lawyers for both sides and other litigation costs. Some of the legal fees translate into several thousands of dollars an hour for services rendered, believe it or not. And you should.

With a civil justice system like that, no wonder justice is said to be blind: She might not like a lot of the things being done in her name if she could see them up close and personal.

Within a half century, the U.S. tort system has gone from being a powerful protector of individual liberty guaranteed by the *Rule of Law* into a court-sponsored, get-rich-quick scheme that rewards self-interest, discourages freedom, and engenders fear and suspicion throughout society.

Over the years, the U.S. tort system has become a much abused process perpetuated by well paid lobbyists with lawyers and law firms funneling recycled "lottery" money into political contributions aimed at protecting the vested interests of America's rich and powerful trial attorneys.

What the trial lawyers have fashioned is an out-of-control civil justice system made possible by misguided jurists who interpret the law in ways that facilitate America's self-destructing litigation explosion without regard to its consequences.

Many of these lawyers and judges would argue, however, that the tort system is alive and well in America. They undoubtedly would argue that the U.S. tort system was designed to protect the rights of the public and that it does just that. And they are right—up to a point. They also would argue that contingent fee attorneys—those who work for a piece of the action, usually a third of it, but sometimes more—enable a segment of society to have access to a system of legal redress that might otherwise be denied them because of cost. That is also true—to a point.

If that were all that mattered—protecting individual rights and assuring universal access to a system of legal redress—then it would make sense that some jurists actually believe the tort system works well. *But that is not **all** that matters.* Far from it.

Eroding Rule of Law

There are serious adverse social, economic and political consequences that must be weighed on the scales of justice against the actual value derived by society from *assigning* blame in civil disputes.

The economic cost of the litigious society on America's infrastructure is huge, almost unfathomable. But it is only one cost. And it pales when compared to the terrible social cost *the lawsuit lottery* is having on the *Rule of Law* and the character of the people the law is supposed to protect.

There are many reasons why America grew great and strong for the better part of two centuries. One of the most important, surely, is that for most of our history, this nation functioned as a *meritocracy.*

Our Founding Fathers envisioned America as a new type of country, where there would be "freedom and justice for all." A country without kings, emperors or other tyrannical rulers, and one designed to protect liberty, not take it away.

America, as conceived, would be a "nation of laws" under which the people would rule themselves. This is why the *Rule of Law*—the rules of behavior by which we all abide—was of paramount concern to the Founding Fathers. The *Rule of Law,* with its concept of due process, is what guarantees freedom for each and every American.

Functioning properly, the *Rule of Law* gives citizens, like no other country in history, the freedom to act, to take risks, to make free choices—and to be held accountable for those actions.

It was the *Rule of Law* that gave us the freedom to take the risks needed to succeed or not, as the case may be. It allowed Americans to dream and to achieve those dreams through individual effort. It is what earned Americans a well-deserved reputation for "rugged individualism."

The *Rule of Law* gave Americans confidence that they knew right from wrong and the courage to act accordingly, knowing the *Rule of Law* would defend their reasonable choices.

It was America's willingness to take risks that became a defining feature of our national culture. We have seen it in the greatness of our nation's innovators and leaders, and in their resourcefulness and ingenuity. We observed it in science, business, education, industry, finance, and in government.

This uniquely American "can do" attitude permeated every sector of American society. We *acquired* it not by wondering "Why?" but by asking, "Why not?" And we *earned* our reputation for rugged individualism by having faith in ourselves and taking personal responsibility for the choices and risks we made—having pride in those actions that proved successful, while learning from experiences that did not.

It was the *Rule of Law* that enabled a nation of poor immigrants to evolve into the richest, most powerful country in history.

It was the *Rule of Law* and the freedom it engendered that gave our nation unparalleled stability, that distinguished America from all other nations, that attracted international respect and huge amounts of investment from friendly countries around the world.

For almost 200 years, Americans relied on the *certainty* of the *Rule of Law* to define our individual rights and freedoms. We submitted to it without trepidation. It was the *Rule of Law* that gave America both national and international legitimacy.

But something changed in the mid-20th century that seriously threatens that legitimacy.

For whatever reasons—and one can speculate about any number of them—the peculiarly American qualities of individualism, self-reliance, and fearlessness began to erode.

Perhaps America had grown so great and so powerful that by the end of World War II we, as a nation, gradually began to reflect the truth in the adage about "absolute power corrupting absolutely."

Or perhaps it was that we began to lose touch with those great nation-building attributes that helped turn individual hopes, dreams and aspirations into collective realities.

Or maybe it was America's failure to heed William Gladstone's 150-year-old admonition about too much justice being "the surest road to national downfall."

Chances are that all these scenarios have been contributing to the deterioration of the *Rule of Law* in America and to the gradual disintegration of the greatness that once defined America's character.

Whatever the reasons, in just two generations, the U.S. civil justice system has reversed course.

No longer does it protect individual rights as intended by our Founding Fathers. Instead it *threatens* the rights of all Americans with too much law and too much of what nowadays goes for justice.

With the number of tort cases at about 20 million a year, going to court has been adopted as the weapon of choice for solving civil disputes.

Where once our courts denigrated lawsuits in favor of reasonableness and personal accountability, they now encourage wholesale litigation.

Instead of protecting rights, our courts today revel in blame mongering, doling out punishment with abandon in the misguided belief that unrestricted litigation is the surest road to social utopia.

So perverse has America's civil litigation system become that nobody has any idea of what a court will do.

We now find our courts punishing even the innocent while extravagantly rewarding the frivolous and irresponsible whose self-centered philosophy can best be described as, "None for all and all for one."

We have gone from being the land of the free to the home of the over-lawed, over-ruled and over-regulated.

We have seen our courtrooms transformed into debating platforms, where the best argument often holds the greatest sway with emotion-driven judges and juries, the facts notwithstanding.

And we have watched courtroom civility all but disappear as an evolving breed of entrepreneurial lawyers becomes increasingly aggressive, adversarial and predatory, sometimes even employing improprieties to win as much as they can, as often as they can and at all costs.

LEGITIMACY UNDERMINED

The ultimate tragedy of the sense of victimization and entitlement that now permeates the American psyche is the worsening effect it is having on the diminution of the *Rule of Law.*

Where once the public, the business world and the international community understood and trusted the American *Rule of Law,* they now fear its uncertainty. The potential social and economic consequences of that fear are grave, indeed.

Once a nation of risk takers, fear and suspicion now condition our every action and interaction—in business, healthcare, education, government—on the street, in the workplace, even in church and at home.

Fear of liability is stifling America's ingenuity and resourcefulness. It squashes people's freedom to act; and it saps the nation's willingness to take risks. Our once unbounded desire to succeed has been replaced by fear of failure as America's primary driving force.

As Philip K. Howard points out in his book, *The Collapse of the Common Good,* "Doing something wrong is not what scares most Americans. What we're afraid of is someone claiming we did."

For whatever reasons—let the sociologists figure them out—America has become a nation of self-centered, self-anointed "victims" that readily lay blame for their failures and deficiencies on others. This particularly pernicious trait has been spreading throughout the population like a virulent cancer.

Yes, let the sociologists figure it out. But in the meantime, isn't it curious how Americans began acting as though they were entitled to other people's money about the time the federal government began treating the public to entitlements for which citizens once felt personally responsible.

Those so-called government entitlements now account for more than half the federal budget. Then again, maybe it's a bit of a stretch to think the government would condition Americans to be dependent upon it, much like Pavlov did with dogs. Then again—maybe it's not that much of a stretch.

As Charles Sykes, author of *A Nation of Victims*, assessed it: "We want to be a pain-free, no-fault, no-guilt society." The real victims, Sykes goes on to say, "tend to get lost in the shuffle." Applying Sykes' observation to today's blame-based U.S. tort system, we can readily understand how monstrously unjust and harmful *the lawsuit lottery* has become.

Today we live in a culture that has almost religiously discarded "assumption of risk" and the principle of personal responsibility in favor of a seemingly universal predisposition for victimization and a growing sense of entitlement to compensation for every wrong that comes our way.

Litigation is now the option of first choice whenever something goes awry. The lawsuit has become society's favorite remedy for a failed life, a job gone wrong, any disagreement, or a marriage that fails. Accidents are no longer "accidents"; they have become green lights for lawsuits.

While the U.S. tort system may not be the *cause* of society's growing sense of victimization, it most assuredly validates and exacerbates the public's growing sense of entitlement to the wealth of others.

Consider this: Fifty years ago, if a youngster stumbled and cut himself on a rusty nail while playing at night in a vacant lot, his parents most likely scolded him for playing where he shouldn't have been, while seeking medical treatment. Today, the same scenario would likely result in a prompt call to a personal injury lawyer probably *before* seeking medical treatment—and that lawyer would gleefully rattle off the names of a half-dozen or so potential defendants, none the least of which would be the manufacturer of the rusty nail that did the damage.

The metamorphosis in American character occurred not overnight but incrementally—as government and business grew bigger and more dominant in the aftermath of World War II.

At the same time, the public sensed a loss of individual power in what was becoming an increasingly over-regulated society.

Fear of vulnerability and feelings of victimization followed suit, manifesting itself in the meteoric rise in litigation for every misunderstanding, accident or other misfortune that came along.

Whereas Americans once willingly accepted responsibility for their own actions and choices, the public gradually came to believe that every bad thing should be blamed on someone or something. And whoever or whatever contributed in any way to any bad thing must be made to pay. *The lawsuit lottery* became the most popular way to get that payment.

Instead of earning our way in the *meritocracy* that America once was, we have allowed society's mettle to rust from selfishness and opportunism. The powerlessness and fear the public first began sensing 50 years ago has grown steadily into a senseless rage of entitlement that has all but destroyed the *meritocracy* envisioned by our Founding Fathers.

With civil justice becoming synonymous with self-interest, many judges no longer "judge" the sense of law in their courtrooms.

Instead, they have become tort tax assessors, assigning blame based on competing theories of liability, while facts are played like pawns in this adversarial game.

We have seen the legal profession's ethical rules against stirring litigation all but evaporate. We have watched legal procedures that once made litigation difficult to even contemplate evaporate to a point where little more than the urge to sue is required to file a lawsuit.

We have seen the *Rule of Law* devolve into a shadow of its former self—too often arbitrary, sometimes unjust, but always fearsome in the uncertainty created by too much law and the diminution of judicial authority.

This is not to say that the U.S. tort system is evil or unnecessary. Quite the contrary. In its once laudable form, the tort system's purpose was to right "wrongs" and to protect the public against what Shakespeare called "the evil that men do." But the system has changed.

One of the best arguments against what it has become was voiced 235 years ago by Samuel Adams, who wrote, "… what a man has honestly acquired is absolutely his own, which he may freely give, but cannot be taken away from him without his consent."

As originally designed, the tort system provided a systematic way to resolve civil disputes based on a sense of the common good and to protect the public against unsafe products and practices, and professional incompetence. No one quarrels with those goals, least of all the authors of this book.

But, the tort system has been corrupted over time. Plaintiffs today are abdicating responsibility for *their own conduct,* abetted by unrestrained attorneys who gravely exploit the system as they prowl for a buck, often without regard to the merit of their cases or the grossly excessive economic harm they cause.

As for protecting the rights of Americans, the most important "right" Americans appear to care about today is the right to sue—which doesn't exist except in our own selfish mind-set.

It is unbridled selfishness that has caused America's civil justice system to deteriorate to where it now provides too much justice. And, as Jean Racine predicted in the 17th century, with too much justice, *injustice* is assured.

Not to put too cynical a point on it, but the effect of the tort tax on America and Americans can best be summarized by the ironic words of Walt Kelly in his *Pogo* comic strip: "We have met the enemy, and he is us."

Chapter 6

... Protecting Your Assets

*"It is of great importance in a republic not only to guard against
the oppression of its rulers, but to guard one part of society
against the injustice of the other part."*

—Alexander Hamilton (1755–1804)
U.S. Secretary of Treasury

About a half century ago, while the United States was planting Minuteman missiles in backyard silos, Americans by the thousands were building personal bomb shelters against possible nuclear attack. In all, more than a hundred thousand citizens built bunkers, afraid that the Cold War strategy of "mutually assured destruction" might not work.

Little did they know that, while trying to protect themselves against an *external* threat to America, a different kind of *internal* threat loomed on the horizon. This new enemy, as *Pogo* suggested, is "us," the American people. And the threat we pose to each other is gnawing away at our nation's economic strength and moral fiber. The weapon used is litigation—wholesale litigation, with Americans suing Americans for all they can get.

ASSET PROTECTION PLANNING

So destabilizing is this ceaseless attack on America's wealth and character that the "fear of liability has become the defining feature of our culture," according to the noted lawyer-author, Philip K. Howard.

The "culture of fear" Howard warned about (and the dysfunctional tort system that nurtures it) prompted a small group of attorneys about a dozen years ago to find ways to help protect their clients' assets from *the lawsuit lottery.*

What these lawyers devised was a sort of "legal bunker"—a stop-gap reaction to predatory litigation that uses existing law in creative ways to legally shield assets against the abuse of law that now dominates the U.S. tort system. It's called Comprehensive Asset Protection Planning or CAPP.

As a result, individuals fearful of liability now have a number of pro-active options available that, when used in combination, help even the odds that are otherwise stacked against defendants in today's U.S. tort system.

The most important of these lines of defense are: liability insurance, mandatory arbitration (some legal eagles like to call it, Alternate Dispute Resolution or ADR) and a series of artfully crafted legal tools that provide a hard-to-crack shield against the threat of litigation.

So successful has this type of planning been that increasing numbers of Americans have begun adopting asset protection strategies in recent years.

A survey by *The Wall Street Journal* showed that 35% of those with more than $1 million in assets had some form of asset protection in place in 2003. That compares to 17% in 2000. Of those still without asset protection, 61% said they were interested in creating a plan, according to the *Journal.*

Another survey—this one reported in *Trusts & Estates* magazine—confirms the public's growing interest in asset protection. Conducted by Prince & Associates, the survey questioned 227 private-client lawyers, a majority of whom said fear of litigation and high divorce rates caused many clients to be "very" or "extremely" interested in asset protection planning.

Importantly, the P&A study also concluded that, while the lawyers surveyed are interested in asset protection, most are apprehensive about it—probably, they admit, because of unfamiliarity with this relatively new field of law and—perhaps, even more importantly—because they know so little about how to create an asset protection plan. Of the lawyers surveyed, only 16.3% described themselves as authorities on asset protection planning; 73.6% of them said they needed to know more about it.

Despite apprehension and their lack of knowledge about the basics of asset protection, two-thirds of the lawyers surveyed said they expect asset protection to play an increasing role in their law practices in the future.

All of which points to a growing need for the public and, most particularly, the legal profession to better understand what asset protection is all about, what it can and can't do, and why it does what it does.

Some of the following scenarios may help illustrate how comprehensive asset protection planning works, realizing that any of these circumstances may become a reality for any one of us at any time.

The best scenario, of course, is that a lawsuit never materializes, or, if it does, that it goes away for whatever reason.

Perhaps the plaintiff has a change of mind—or a pang of conscience; or the plaintiff's lawyer concludes the case is too weak or too problematic. Or, as it may happen, the mere presence of an asset protection plan provides enough muscle to scare off the attackers.

ALTERNATIVE DISPUTE RESOLUTION

If a dispute does materialize, the first line of defense in a comprehensive asset protection plan is to try to nip the complaint in the bud, *before* it gets out of hand and explodes into a lawsuit.

This is where a well-drafted arbitration agreement or employment policy with workers, vendors, patients, other business colleagues, even family members, can be worth its weight in gold. Why? Because arbitration works. It provides a viable alternative to lawsuits.

The American Arbitration Association estimates that 80% to 90% of the disputes it mediates and/or arbitrates are quickly and cost-effectively resolved *without* litigation.

While the specifics of mandatory mediation/arbitration plans can vary from user to user, in general, most plans require the parties to attempt to resolve disputes *informally* before seeking an independent mediator to help negotiate a settlement without imposing one. If mediation fails, the process then moves forward to independent arbitration, where the arbitrator's decision most often is final and binding, though not always, depending on the terms of the arbitration plan.

Mandatory arbitration first came on the scene during the 1970s. Since then, Alternative Dispute Resolution programs—or ADR, as human resource professionals like to call it—has become an immensely popular way of handling disagreements and other forms of conflict out-of-court.

So popular is arbitration today that it can be found burgeoning in virtually every public and private sector of society. In business... finance... education... government... healthcare...just about everywhere!

Many banks and credit card companies now require an arbitration agreement with their customers as a matter of course. Schools require teachers to sign them. You may not be able to buy a car or get telephone service without agreeing to one. Try seeing a doctor, and you may be asked to sign an arbitration agreement; refuse and you may be asked to find another doctor.

As might be expected, the most explosive growth in the use of mandatory arbitration comes from employers looking for a strong deterrent against the overwhelming amount of litigation being filed by disgruntled workers regarding such job-related matters as age discrimination, sexual harassment, retaliation and wrongful termination, just to name a few of the more prominent complaints.

Even the courts themselves and countless law firms have begun insisting that employees agree to arbitrate contentious issues instead of resorting to more costly and time-consuming litigation. *(That's sort of like not allowing others to do unto you what you do to others, isn't it?)*

Growth in the number of employers in the private sector using arbitration has been increasing steadily for years—up from an estimated 3.6% in 1991 to 19% in 1997, according to *Dispute Resolution Journal.*

By 1998, about 62% of all large corporations had used employment arbitration at least once. And in the four years ended 2001, the number of employees covered by employment arbitration plans administered by the American Arbitration Association had grown from 3-million to 6-million. Moreover, during the five-year period ended in 2001, the AAA reported a three-fold increase in its caseload to about 225,000 a year.

One need not look too far to find the motive behind the accelerating use of job-related ADRs in America: Employment disputes represent one of the fastest growing areas in law today.

Confronted with a tidal wave of job-related litigation, employers have become a modern-day proof of Newton's Third Law of Motion, which teaches that there is an equal and opposite reaction for every action. Mandatory arbitration is just such a reaction. What's more, ADR is cheaper, swifter, with more reliable resolutions than court trials; it's more confidential and less stressful than any lawsuit imaginable. And when the arbitration process is over, relationships tend not to be as frayed as they can get in a courtroom.

According to Vivian Berger, professor *emerita* at Columbia University Law School and a practicing mediator, the best ADR programs are those that, among other things, subsidize the cost of mediation and permit the employee's lawyer to attend the mediation sessions.

The AAA goes farther than that. It will not agree to administer any arbitration request if the employer does not pay *all* employee costs, other than a nominal administrative fee of no more than $125.

The consensus is that the most effective corporate ADR plans are scrupulously fair and focused on problem solving, not assessing blame, with all sides having the same rights, obligations and risks. What the courts generally look for in employment-related ADR is whether a plan is unconscionable, lopsided or overreaching in favor of the employer—and whether the employee has been required to relinquish any important rights by the arbitration plan.

The fact is that workplace arbitration plans have been under close court scrutiny almost from the beginning. They have been the subject of three major U.S. Supreme Court decisions in the past 10 years, encouraging employment law scholar Charles Craver of George Washington University Law School to conclude that the highest court of the land clearly favors arbitration in many areas.

Many attribute the Supreme Court's 2001 ruling in *Circuit City Stores, Inc. v. Adams* which stated that binding arbitration can be a condition of employment, as triggering the upsurge in demand for arbitration services that is now sweeping the country.

Other courts have also studied the issue. The always adventuresome 9th Circuit Court of Appeals, for instance, has examined the subject repeatedly, ruling first one way, then another, including among its decisions that employers "may require employees to sign agreements to arbitrate Title VII claims as a condition of employment." (Title VII of the Civil Rights Act covers many of the workplace discrimination disputes that ADR employment agreements and policies address.)

As one might expect, mandatory arbitration has not been without its critics. Employee advocates complain that corporate arbitration plans don't afford the worker a level playing field. What employee advocates really are complaining about is that the arbitration playing field *is* level, as it should be—not like the one in litigation, which greatly favors the plaintiff.

In all fairness, however, there may be some truth to this criticism with respect to some ADR plans that may be overbearing—but not nearly enough to throw the baby out with the bath water, as some advocates suggest.

Plans that lean the wrong way in favor of the employer are likely to self-destruct in any event when it comes to the question of enforceability, if challenged in court.

There is, of course, no surprise at all when trial lawyers complain about arbitration. That's to be expected. After all, arbitration competes directly with *the lawsuit lottery*—especially the settlement phase, when lawyers are very much in charge of the negotiating process. Not so with ADR, where the arbitrators have no vested interest whatsoever in the outcome.

When trial lawyers put forth that kind of disingenuous criticism, one is reminded of the story about the lawyer who sneeringly patronized a witness on the stand in a courtroom, saying, "You seem to have the average share of intelligence for a man of your background." To which the witness replied, "If I wasn't under oath, I'd return the compliment."

LIABILITY INSURANCE

The second line of defense in the comprehensive asset protection planning process is liability insurance.

If arbitration fails and/or a lawsuit does materialize, the legal team afforded by liability insurance will more than likely assume the role of the insured's lawyers.

(One should never forget, however, that the focus of an insurer's lawyers is always the *insurer's* best interests. Mindful of that, it is not unheard of for a defendant to hire an attorney to oversee an insurer's defense team.)

Fortunately, most of us have some level of insurance coverage for the obvious potential liabilities, such as automobile insurance, homeowner's insurance, professional liability coverage and directors and officers insurance.

As much insurance as we may have, however, chances are it probably won't cover *all* potential liabilities. And whatever coverage we do have will be limited not only by dollar amount but also, in all probability, by exclusions.

Sometimes, believe it or not, some of those exclusions are found in the small print buried deep within the legalese of the actual policy.

The fact is we are all vulnerable to all sorts of lawsuits that traditional insurance may not cover, e.g., discrimination, sexual harassment, wrongful termination, etc. You name it.

Unfortunately, if liability insurance fails to cover the type of complaint involved (sexual discrimination, for example), the defendant may be held personally accountable for the entire settlement or judgment reached—which can be costly. (Note that 67% of sexual discrimination cases end in the plaintiff's favor; the mean jury award for sexual discrimination climbed to $529,373 in 2000, according to *Jury Verdict Research*.)

If liability insurance *does* cover the complaint but *not* the entire amount of the settlement or judgment, the defendant may be held responsible for any amount in excess of the insurer's obligation. (This, too, can be costly, considering that average jury awards skyrocketed past $1.2 million in 2002. The average award for medical malpractice is three times that amount.)

Insurance premiums also can be extremely expensive, particularly for frequently targeted high-risk professionals, such as physicians.

Incidentally, lawyers are far from immune to legal attack for malpractice. In 2002, there were 35,000 claims of legal malpractice, about one-third of which resulted in awards or judgments for the plaintiffs. The large majority of the claims were against lawyers with more than 10 years of experience. (The number of negligence claims against lawyers was actually greater since these statistics refer only to claims against *insured* lawyers.)

Even more shocking is the estimate that lawyers, whose malpractice premiums also have been spiraling upward in recent years, can expect to be sued about three times during their careers—a trend that many anti-lawyer cynics doubtlessly consider poetic justice!

So expensive has liability insurance become that more and more professionals, faced with unaffordable premiums, are opting to self-insure, which is risky business, indeed. A growing number of doctors are doing just that—practicing medicine *without malpractice insurance,* relying instead on the threat of bankruptcy to ward off exorbitant patient claims.

So pronounced is the self-insurance trend in Florida that one local wealth management firm reports that 60% of its physician-clients were practicing without insurance in 2003 because of the high cost and coverage limitations of malpractice policies; whereas, ten years ago, only 20% of the firm's client-base was self-insured.

Even more startling is a *Wall Street Journal* report that more than one out of 20 active Florida physicians are going "bare," a tendency that may be spreading to other states. The *Journal* also reports that, "Many of the doctors dropping malpractice insurance are sheltering assets in sophisticated trusts or partnerships, safely out of reach from legal judgments down the road."

While sympathizing with the depth of frustration that leads to that kind of draconian thinking, liability insurance, as costly as it is, nonetheless should be included in any comprehensive asset protection plan if at all possible and to the fullest extent practicable to get the most benefit from the planning.

In short, it is risky business to go without *some* level of insurance coverage—nor should anyone be lulled into believing that such coverage will provide enough protection to do the whole job. It may not.

ELIMINATING INCENTIVE TO SUE

When all else fails, the third line of defense against lawsuits involves the legal tools that become a carefully crafted part of any comprehensive asset protection plan.

What these tools do in effect is build a legal fortress around a client's vulnerable assets, placing them, when necessary, in legal jurisdictions well beyond the reach of predator attorneys and law-suit-happy plaintiffs.

These legal tools, along with the jurisdictions and strategies selected by an experienced asset protection attorney, are crafted in ways that accomplish two primary objectives. The first is to make it difficult or nearly impossible for would-be creditors to collect judgments against an individual's personal wealth. The second and equally important objective is to substantially enhance the individual's negotiating strength when attempting to settle *legitimate* disputes.

What asset protection attorneys strive to do is use the law to eliminate the incentive to sue and to do it long before the threat of a lawsuit arises. This is done, typically, by *removing the remedy* of a lawsuit. That's lawyer-talk for separating the client from the legal title to what every plaintiff wants from a defendant's estate—namely, the defendant's money and whatever else can be converted into cash.

Thus the value of asset protection planning comes from its formidable ability to deny unwanted access to a client's otherwise vulnerable assets—without denying the client beneficial ownership of, or distributive rights to, those assets.

One approach commonly used in asset protection planning is to creatively weave together a series of increasingly protective shields, typically two or three legal tools, each of which already exists for other purposes, such as estate planning, general corporate ownership, etc.

Selection of the right mix of tools depends largely on the individual's financial circumstances and desired level of asset protection.

FAMILY LIMITED PARTNERSHIP

While attorneys have developed a variety of asset protection methodologies, most plans have a similar look and feel.

Most asset protection plans, for instance, include a limited partnership, which is the core of asset protection. There may be one or more limited liability companies (LLCs) owned by the partnership, plus the ultimate lawsuit deterrent—an international asset protection trust (APT) which, in a comprehensive asset protection plan, owns the partnership and thus any related LLCs.

The limited partnership often is called the Family Limited Partnership or FLP because spouses and other family members tend to be the organizing partners. It is the most popular and cost-effective *domestic* form of asset protection, particularly for those with a net worth under $250,000. The FLP also is the primary tool used to create the legal barrier between the assets, the owner of the assets, and whoever would try to take them away.

Operated as a business with its own tax identification number, the FLP is given legal title to the client's so-called "safe assets"—those that are not likely to hurt anyone, such as cash, stocks and bonds, art and other collectibles. In most cases, these safe assets comprise the bulk of a client's estate. The FLP also may own and operate one or more limited liability companies or other corporate entities.

Organizationally, the Family Limited Partnership must have at least two partners: typically, a 1% or 2% general partner who has complete control over the partnership's assets; and a limited partner or partners (generally, the client and co-client spouse and perhaps other family members). The limited partners account for the partnership's remaining ownership.

While not responsible for paying taxes, the FLP is required to file a Form 1065 annually with the Internal Revenue Service. It must also distribute a report of partnership income to the partners for inclusion in their individual state and federal income tax returns. In plans that include an Asset Protection Trust, a copy of the K-1 also would go to the "Settlor" of the Trust.

Only the general partner has personal liability in the partnership, which is why risky assets should not be placed in an FLP. As long as the limited partners exert no control over the partnership's assets, limited partners are protected from personal liability with respect to the use of those assets.

As for the assets themselves, they derive protection by being owned not by an individual but by the partnership. As such, the assets typically would not be named in a lawsuit against one of the partners.

An FLP's biggest lawsuit deterrence is that it usually is registered in a state where the court's "charging order" is "the sole and exclusive remedy" for a creditor to collect a judgment from a debtor-partner. (The most popular partnership-friendly states are Arizona, Nevada and Delaware.) Typically, a creditor's only hope of collecting a judgment from the debtor-partner of an FLP is if and when the partnership opts to *distribute* income or principal to the debtor-partner.

Adding to this already significant deterrence is the prospect that a creditor may be required to report as taxable income any earned but as yet *undistributed* income accrued to the benefit of the debtor-partner. Thus, if a debtor-partner's share of an FLP's earned-but-undistributed income amounts to, say, $25,000, the creditor may have to report that amount as income to the IRS and pay tax on it—even though the creditor has not received it.

In reality, what "charging order" protection does is create an expensive waiting game—one that may prompt a settlement significantly more favorable to the debtor-partner than might otherwise be likely.

LIMITED LIABILITY COMPANY

Unlike the FLP, the function of a Limited Liability Company (LLC) is to separate and compartmentalize the client's "risky" assets into protective "sub-bunkers" owned by the FLP and under the responsibility of the general partner.

Assets relegated to an LLC typically are those that by their very nature possess some inherent potential for harm—for instance, a business activity, investment real estate, rental properties, boats, planes, etc.

Importantly, while the LLC's Articles of Organization *may* be filed in any state, an LLC usually is required to register in the state where it does business and/or its property is located.

Funding the LLC with assets begins only after a federal Employer Identification Number is received from the IRS. All that's required then is to re-title ownership of the risky assets in the name of the appropriate LLC.

Assigning risky assets to one or more LLCs, in effect, legally separates those assets from each other as well as the partnership's safe assets, while at the same time minimizing the owners' over-all potential liability.

Because members of limited liability companies are treated much like shareholders of corporations, they generally cannot be held liable for the acts of an LLC. That's another form of protection afforded by the LLC.

A third level of LLC protection is derived from the fact that, in most cases, the LLC's original member is the partnership. The LLC's assets therefore can readily be liquidated into cash by the general partner and transferred to the increased safety of the plan's partnership or—for even greater safety—uploaded into the asset protection trust.

For income tax purposes, when the only member is the FLP, the limited liability company is treated as a "disregarded entity" and doesn't need a separate tax return. All the accounting is included on the partnership's return. In all other cases, the LLC typically is treated as a partnership for income tax purposes and would file its own 1065 tax return.

INTERNATIONAL ASSET PROTECTION TRUST

For many, the degree of *domestic* asset protection provided by the FLP-LLC combination may not be sufficient, given the amount of risk, the size of the asset base involved and the anticipated tenacity of any predatory attack.

For such clients, the ultimate in lawsuit deterrence is the international Asset Protection Trust, also known as the APT.

In general, people establish APTs to protect (from unanticipated lawsuits and other legal actions) and preserve assets and to ensure the well-being of the beneficiaries.

Relatively new to mainstream law, the international asset protection trust can be particularly beneficial to high-risk, high net worth professionals with deep pockets and substantial vulnerable assets.

There is, however, more than one way to establish the desired jurisdictional protection with an international asset protection trust. Some asset protection lawyers, for instance, prefer to create a trust without a family limited partnership. They opt instead to internationalize the Trust from the get go and immediately relocate the assets to a jurisdiction outside the U.S.

A far less expensive but equally effective and more flexible alternative is to pair an asset protection trust with a family limited partnership and one or more LLCs, and to internationalize the Trust *only* if and when the assets are threatened. Until then, the assets would never have to leave the U.S. and would remain in the domestic FLP unless the Trust is triggered.

The primary purpose of the APT is to "own" the family limited partnership and, through it, any LLCs in the asset protection plan. If and when a crisis hits, the APT can be quickly internationalized or triggered. If necessary, the assets then can be telescoped up into the APT and removed to the safety of a jurisdiction outside the U.S.

Unless triggered by an "event of duress" (that means a lawsuit or other asset-threatening crisis), the APT typically acts as a U.S. grantor trust for income tax purposes and by the laws of one of the more trust-friendly states, such as Alaska, Delaware, Rhode Island or Nevada.

For all other purposes, the APT usually is governed by the laws of the jurisdiction where the trust is recorded, e.g., the Cook Islands (where such trusts were originally created), Belize, Nevis, or some other country noted for its tough asset protection laws.

Unlike an FLP, an APT may own sub-chapter S stock and annuities, prior to a triggering. The Trust may also own personal residences without loss of related capital gains exclusions or home interest deduction benefits.

In addition, while ERISA qualified retirement accounts—e.g., IRAs, SEPs, and 401(k)s—may not be placed in any asset protection tool, the APT may be a primary or contingent beneficiary of any such plans.

If triggered by a threat to the plan's assets, the APT becomes an international trust, at which time a foreign Successor Trustee or co-Trustee steps in and may transfer the plan's assets to a pre-selected foreign jurisdiction, without loss of beneficial ownership. Once a threat ends, the APT can revert to being a U.S. grantor trust, if desired.

Typically, the mere threat of triggering an international asset protection trust may be sufficient to ward off most predator attorneys and give legitimate creditors pause for thought about settling the matter on more attractive terms than might otherwise be the case.

A particularly determined creditor could, of course, pursue the case to some distant trust-friendly jurisdiction where the chances of penetrating a well-prepared APT, drawn and recorded in accordance with that country's stringent trust laws, have proven to be little to none—and the probable potential cost to the creditor could be substantial.

For one thing, local lawyers must be used; for another, contingent fee attorneys need not apply when it comes to attacking an international asset protection trust—they are not allowed.

Plaintiffs must prove a case in the Cook Islands, for example, by the much higher standard of "beyond a reasonable doubt" vs. "preponderance of the evidence," as required in U.S. courts.

Plaintiffs must also post a bond in the Cook Islands to cover expected court costs, before a case can even be filed. The plaintiff must also pay to fly a judge in from New Zealand to hear the case.

Worse yet for the plaintiff, if a Cook Islands trust has been in existence and funded for more than 2 years, which is the statute of limitations in that country, there is no case.

As to how the assets are administered after an APT is triggered, the Trust's grantor may request distributions of resources to selected beneficiaries and may make bequests through "Letters of Wishes" to the foreign Trustee.

Importantly, the foreign Trustee is bound to the beneficiaries by fiduciary duty and must follow the directions established in the Trust. Accordingly, the foreign Trustee may also make distributions of resources for the maintenance, support, health, education and general welfare of any and all beneficiaries, which may include the grantor.

LEGAL PITFALLS

Tailoring asset protection plans to individual needs is a job that only a skilled and experienced asset protection attorney should attempt, if for no other reason than that the benefits of the strategies employed may be lost if they fail to comply with all applicable state, federal and international laws, as well as any precedents that may have been set by previous court actions.

While high-risk, high net worth individuals are obvious candidates for asset protection planning, in practice just about anyone with assets to lose can benefit from the lawsuit-deterrent effect of asset protection planning. This is particularly true of middle-class Americans, who are finding that even a modest lawsuit has the potential to wipe out a lifetime of accumulated wealth.

Regardless of the net worth involved, there are a number of critical considerations of which both the asset protection attorney and the client should be cognizant. Most critically important is the timing of funding the legal tools with assets. The law is very strict on this point.

Funding may occur *only* when there are no creditor claims pending, threatened or expected. To do otherwise may invite a charge of "fraudulent conveyance," which could result in transactions being overturned—and even more dire consequences, such as prosecution.

Also critically important is that the Settlor of an APT remain solvent *after* funding, with the ability to pay all reasonably anticipated debt from resources outside the Trust. The courts may not look favorably on those partnerships and trusts that are established otherwise.

Considerable estate planning expertise may also be required in the preparation of asset protection plans, since there typically is much linkage with traditional estate planning and retirement tools, such as irrevocable trusts, pensions, life insurance programs, annuities, wills or revocable living trusts.

So there is no misunderstanding, what asset protection planning *doesn't* do—and shouldn't do—is *conceal* assets from legitimate creditors or hide income from the Internal Revenue Service. Unfortunately, some legal beagles and their clients may attempt to do just that. The government has a word for that type of planning, and it's not asset protection. It's fraud.

Unlike schemes that promise huge tax benefits, legitimate asset protection plans are always *income tax neutral.* Their sole objective is to protect assets from abusive litigation—not cheat the government by evading income taxes.

The best advice that can be offered to someone being pitched on the tax-saving benefits of asset protection is to hold on to your wallet and head for the door as fast as you can. Any so-called asset protection plan that purports to save on income taxes is most certainly questionable if not illegal.

What legitimate asset protection does is use the law to prevent the Law's abuse in the U.S. tort system. That's all.

As might be expected, and as alluded to earlier, some jurists take a dim view of asset protection—not because it's unethical, because it is not; and not because it is illegal, because it is not.

Most of whatever criticism there is comes from those who know little or nothing about this relatively new field of law, and much of what is said to be criticism emanates mostly from trial lawyers whose ox may be gored by legitimate asset protection planning.

A typical argument by trial attorneys with vested interests in the financial outcome of *the lawsuit lottery* is that asset protection is a wily way of circumventing the law to avoid claims of future creditors.

If by circumventing the law they mean crafting existing law in ways that create a level playing field where plaintiffs and their predator attorneys no longer have a decidedly unfair advantage, then asset protection attorneys doubtlessly would plead "guilty, as charged."

The fact is that many of the victims in today's civil justice system are the *defendants* who need protecting and *not* the plaintiffs who claim to be victims, without responsibility for their own choices and often irresponsible acts.

Let's also not forget that asset protection would be wholly unnecessary and would most likely fade away if the *Rule of Law* provided the kind of public protection it once did.

And while on the subject of protecting the public, let's not forget the fellow who, when caught embezzling millions, told his lawyer he didn't want to go to jail. The lawyer reassured him, saying: "Don't worry. You'll never have to go to jail with all that money." His lawyer was right. His client didn't have a dime when he went to prison.

Chapter 7

... It's About Reformation

"The worse the society, the more law there will be.
In Hell there will be nothing but law,
and due process will be meticulously observed."

—Grant Gilmore (1910–1982)
Yale Law Professor

It's been said that reformers make colleagues feel miserable about their pleasures. That is undoubtedly true in the case of tort reform, considering the great harm some colleagues have done to the civil justice system and the amount of pleasure they have extracted from the enormous tort tax paid by Americans in *the lawsuit lottery.*

How colleagues feel about tort reform isn't the issue, however, nor is what some well-meaning and passionate reformers felt 50 years ago when deciding that unrestrained litigation would be good for the soul of America.

All that matters is that those decisions and the greed-driven actions of some powerful trial attorneys have proven to be terribly costly to our country in more ways than one might imagine.

What matters is that their decisions and actions spawned a dysfunctional tort system where too much law is practiced and not enough justice is dispensed—and where debilitating fear and economic devastation for many are the only certainties.

What matters is that they have corrupted our civil courts into entrepreneurial machines where selfishness reigns supreme and individual freedoms are not protected but suppressed.

What matters is that the world community is also growing increasingly concerned about the legitimacy of our legal system.

The world community has always been far more sensitive to the issue of American legitimacy than Americans.

For one thing, America is the only country in the developed world that allows lawyers to collect contingent fees and refuses to grant legal fees and costs to the winners of lawsuits.

For another, we have a million lawyers in America, far more lawyers per capita than any other industrialized nation. And they are hard at work cranking out most of the world's litigation.

Today, the world community sees American doctors protesting in the streets over runaway litigation and sky-high insurance premiums. They see the U.S. government asserting its jurisdiction increasingly over companies and citizens with only the most tenuous connections.

They see the life savings of countless individuals being siphoned away by lawsuits. They see hundreds of companies, many of them major corporations, being driven into bankruptcy. They see entire industries going belly up. They see more and more Americans seeking ways to protect their assets against what amounts to expropriation in the nation's civil courts.

Today, the world community senses the fear of liability that blankets our nation. And, they wonder how a legal system that fails to protect its own citizens can protect the rights of others as America extends its economic and political reach into their countries.

They see a huge American company like Microsoft being broken up by the federal government and sued in over 100 consumer state class action lawsuits for no apparent reason other than being so big and so profitable that it must be overcharging everyone. And they wonder how safe their business interests can be in a country that has so few qualms about punishing the primary sources of its national prosperity merely because those companies and industries are immensely successful—and cash rich.

Quite simply, other countries worry about what the diminishment of the *Rule of Law* in America portends for foreign investment here, for international trade in the global economy, and for the continuation of America's economic superiority and superpower status.

With all these concerns, the time most certainly has come to restore sanity to a judicial system that has long-since given up the right to boast of "justice for all" in favor of "justice for *one*, regardless of all."

Needed is reform, *systemic* tort and court reform, from the top down and the bottom up.

Needed is the reestablishment of our civil courts as havens for the *reasonable* redress of *legitimate* disputes, where the *Rule of Law*—which is the backbone of America's legitimacy—once again can be relied upon to dispense justice equitably, and where frivolous and opportunistic attempts to abuse the U.S. tort system can be quickly rebutted and strongly discouraged.

While there have been numerous attempts at tort reform since the 1970s, nothing even approaching serious nationwide reform has taken hold. That's because much depends on the politics involved.

As the late legal scholar Grant Gilmore pointed out in *The Ages of American Law,* "The decisions which most dramatically affect the life of any society are not and never have been made by courts.... These are political decisions, wise or foolish, virtuous or wicked."

Recognizing that every attempt at major reform has its passionate advocates and adversaries, the first step toward tort reform is to *de-politicize* the issue as much as possible—which is no mean task, considering the amount of serious money being poured into the political process to garner support for opposing points of view.

The powerful trial lawyers' lobby so far has been winning the nationwide battle for the wallets and minds of those legislators and elected judges whose "Nay" votes have been holding tort reform in check.

With the billions of dollars extracted by litigators from class actions and other major torts, no one should be surprised to learn that some of it gets recycled into political contributions aimed at protecting the goose that lays their golden eggs.

Nor should it be surprising that lawyers and law firms have been ranked the number one contributor to political campaigns each year since 1990. In fact, lawyers and law firms invested almost $39 million in political contributions during the first ten months of 2003 alone, with the trial lawyers' national political action committee leading the pack.

Nor should it be surprising that the corporate community, led by the U.S. Chamber of Commerce and the American Medical Association, is also hard at work shoveling tons of dollars into the political campaign favoring the nationwide adoption of tort reform.

Despite the powerful tug-of-war between the trial attorneys and the corporate community—and as Herculean a task as it may seem, the politics of tort reform nonetheless must somehow be neutralized—one vote at a time, if necessary, if the imprint of justice is to be found once again in America's civil justice system.

Frankly, tort reform is too important a national issue to be relegated to the typical polarized "conservative vs. liberal" battle pitting the "haves" against the "have-nots."

Unless and until the issue of "What's wrong with the U.S. tort system?" can be elevated above the rhetoric of politics, ideology and greed—and become simply a question of "What's best for America?"—the inevitable end game for a country too-long-devoid of the *Rule of Law* is too dire to contemplate.

In his book *The Collapse of the Common Good*, Philip K. Howard spells out the politics of tort reform about as succinctly as it can be put. "Trial lawyers, who pit Americans against each other so that they can feed on the carnage, preserve the status quo by filling the pockets of political and judicial candidates," Howard says. "Only a popular movement can succeed in breaking the hammerlock that vested interests have on the system." This book is intended to be a step in the hoped-for creation of that "popular movement."

The reforms suggested and described herein are neither conservative nor liberal, nor designed to emasculate the civil justice system. Rather, they are aimed at putting a bad system back on track by fixing what's broken.

This collection of ideas has been compiled and distilled from many interested and authoritative sources. Some have been tried with varying degrees of success; others have just been talked about. All are offered for one purpose only: To stimulate awareness, discussion and debate, and ultimately to energize some measure of effective reform.

POLITICAL PRESSURE

The reality is that meaningful tort reform *requires* constant and ever-increasing pressure for *nonpartisan* support upon all levels of appropriate authority, from the top down.

That means garnering as much commitment as possible to *system* reform, not just tort reform, in the White House, the U.S. Congress, in every state legislature, in the courts and the legal profession—and in the nation's law schools, where the ethical compass that guides tomorrow's lawyers and judges is being assembled today.

That means building an ever-widening base of support for system reform by adding one politician at a time, one judge at a time, one lawyer at a time, and one law professor at a time, if that's the only way to get the job done. In political terms, system reform is a numbers game. Only when the balance of power shifts politically toward reform will the pressure to end *the lawsuit lottery* begin to take hold nationally.

By any measure, system reform is a hard sell, considering the political realities created by the huge competing war chest made available through the lawyers' lobbyists and from the coffers of corporate America. This, undoubtedly, is why federal efforts to place reasonable limitations on civil liability have been stymied time and again.

LEGISLATIVE REFORM

In recent years, for example, the U.S. House of Representatives repeatedly passed legislation that would have shifted responsibility for many class-action lawsuits from plaintiff-favoring state courts to federal courts—only to find the bills dying in the Senate.

One bill would have given federal courts jurisdiction over class actions when at least 100 members are involved, the total amount of claims exceeds $5 million, and citizens from different states are on opposing sides.

Even as physicians and other healthcare providers staged highly publicized work stoppages and rallies across the country demanding liability reform, the U.S. Senate failed to pass medical liability legislation that had previously been approved by the House. Less than a year later, the Senate again killed another bill that would have imposed limits on jury awards in malpractice cases.

Clearly, the line of rhetorical battle for and against tort reform in Congress has been well delineated.

On the pro side of the issue, congressional tort reformers complain about the political influence of the trial lawyers' lobby in blocking meaningful legislation, while the favorite smokescreen of their opponents is that federal tort reform would encroach on state rights.

Public debate has been no less simplistic or disingenuous.

One of the leaders in the massive lawsuits against the tobacco companies, for instance, Washington trial attorney John P. Coale, had the chutzpah to describe congressional efforts at tort reform as a giveaway to corporate America and the nation's insurance companies, notwithstanding the fact that any such legislation would, among other things, limit his and other tortster fees to about $1,000 an hour—monumentally less than many mass tortsters typically receive.

The U.S. Chamber of Commerce and the AMA, on the other hand and with equal simplicity and glibness, strongly endorse federal legislation because it would, for one thing, deter abusive and frivolous class action lawsuits. The Chamber also argues that multi-state class action suits belong in federal court, "where the rules are the same for everyone."

Both arguments are typical of what we have come to expect from the principal adversaries in the political process. They focus on their own limited interests, namely, money—getting more of it from defendants or giving less of it to plaintiffs. Neither argument deals even remotely with the fundamental issue at stake— *the decline and fall of Justice in America and the great harm the existing civil justice system is causing American society as a whole.*

Unless and until partisanship and greed can be put aside and all parties refocus the argument about tort reform from "What's in it for me?" to "What's in it for America?," that argument will continue to remain just that, an argument with little or no hope of effective resolution.

In that event, the loser quite clearly will be America.

Not only is the battle for tort reform being fought in Washington, D.C., it is also being waged state by state throughout the country.

State legislatures have been fighting for tort reform for years, with somewhat better success than the U.S. Congress.

There have been dozens of laws passed by states eager to alleviate the devastating economic damage caused by the unending tidal wave of personal injury lawsuits, class actions and medical malpractice litigation, only to see many of their efforts circumvented by courts and politics.

Some states have tried to limit the contingency fees charged by lawyers, hoping to dampen the greed-induced incentive to sue. Others have attempted to cap punitive and non-economic damages for un-measurable "pain and suffering."

Disappointingly, of about 25 state legislatures that have passed laws capping non-economic damages in medical liability cases, eleven of them were subsequently overturned in courts on appeal.

Undaunted, other state legislatures—driven by grassroots pressure—continue to seek ways to cure the increasingly abusive tort system, particularly the worsening malpractice disease that afflicts America's financially-wobbly healthcare system.

Even Alabama, reacting to the medical malpractice crisis, reformed its once infamous tort system. Nevada and Florida, among others, have done the same. Texas tried to cap medical malpractice liability as long ago as 1988, but the State Supreme Court shot it down.

Fifteen years later, Texans voted again. This time it was the *citizens* of Texas who voted to change the state constitution in ways that would permit legislative limits on *any* civil action, not just medical malpractice.

The amendment to the Texas Constitution set a $750,000 cap on non-economic damages in medical malpractice lawsuits and limited awards against individual doctors to $250,000. The amendment also empowers lawmakers to set limits on *all* types of lawsuits beginning in 2005.

In Mississippi, described by some as having been one of the most tort-friendly states in the country, lawmakers—in a special session called by the governor—overwhelmingly approved substantial limits on medical malpractice lawsuits. The state acted only after many doctors, dentists and other healthcare professionals threatened to relocate their medical practices to nearby Louisiana, where liability limitations are in effect.

Among other things, the new Mississippi legislation capped non-economic damages at $500,000 until 2010, increasing it to $750,000 in 2011 and $1 million in 2017.

Mississippi also reformed the way financial liability is apportioned among multiple defendants. Under the new law, defendants would be held responsible only for their share of economic damages. Previously, if found to be as little as 5% at fault, physicians could be ordered to pay as much as 50% of a judgment.

The new Mississippi legislation also requires lawsuits to be filed in the county where the alleged malpractice occurred, putting a crimp in the tendency to shop for the most favorable court venues.

One could almost hear a sigh of relief as the president of the Mississippi State Medical Association commented on that state's new legislation: "We're happy," he said. "It affords an opportunity for insurance companies [those that had abandoned the state] to come back into Mississippi."

Less than enthusiastic about the new Mississippi law was the state's Trial Lawyers Association. It issued a statement suggesting that caps on damages would not deter frivolous lawsuits. The trial lawyers organization went on to describe the new Mississippi law as "a rigid, draconian measure that penalizes the most egregiously injured citizens who need our system."

Not clarified in the statement was whether the "egregiously injured citizens" were malpractice lawyers, whose fees are being limited, or the plaintiffs.

COURT REFORM

The kind of institutional change needed requires much more than just legislative reform. It also requires court reform, as well as reform of those aspects of the legal profession that allow greed-driven entrepreneurial pursuits to determine what the practice of law is all about.

One reform of significant importance that has been suggested would be the creation of "special" courts to hear cases involving highly specialized and often conflicting expertise. Such courts would be assigned, for example, to adjudicate malpractice cases, with experts rather than a typical jury empanelled to assess testimony regarding malpractice claims and to determine appropriate judgments.

In the case of medical malpractice, it is believed special courts composed of medical experts would, as a by-product benefit, result in fewer healthcare mistakes by doctors who would be more willing to talk about perceived errors in order to initiate corrective action.

Other important suggested federal and state legislative reforms have already been discussed but are nonetheless worth repeating.

Federal jurisdiction, for example, should be expanded to include multi-state class action lawsuits, with provisions that prevent shopping for tort-friendly courts and ban the consolidation of unrelated claims.

Federal guidelines also should be established to ensure that tort rules are the same for everyone, including a universal statute of limitations for filing tort complaints, limitations on attorneys' fees, and a formula for capping non-economic and punitive damages at some reasonable multiple of actual economic damages sustained.

While not necessarily an indicator of things to come, the U.S. Supreme Court began singing an encouraging tune about tort reform early in 2003, when, in *Campbell v. State Farm*, the court limited a jury's ability to set punitive damages at extremely high multiples of actual economic damages.

The Supreme Court's action is certainly a good omen. It's a first step, perhaps, in establishing an important trend. One can always hope!

To the extent federal law fails to cap tort liability at reasonable levels, however, states legislatures should do it themselves (as they did in Mississippi), including setting reasonable limitations on non-economic and punitive damages.

States should make certain that the funding of legal expenses by champerty is outlawed *de facto* as well as *de jure*. Champerty, a criminal offense in English Common Law, involves third-party investment in the financial outcome of lawsuits. While not lawful in this country, it is believed to be widely practiced with a wink and a nod.

The simplest way for legislators to eliminate the mountain of frivolous lawsuits that clog the nation's courts with greed-induced opportunism and triviality would be to ban the two most terrible tools in torts. That means eliminating the use of contingent fees that make attorneys entrepreneurial partners in lawsuits, and the "no loser pays" feature that encourages filing dubious lawsuits.

Combined, these two features permit some of the most egregious abuses in the U.S. tort system, while encouraging the debilitating spread of America's lawsuit mentality.

Trial attorneys would rather die (or at least spend lots of their tort-raised money) fighting any attempt to eliminate contingent fees and/or the "no loser pays" feature of the U.S. tort system. Why? Easy answer. That's how trial attorneys make most of their big paychecks. And they can do it with little downside risk.

That's not the answer you are likely to hear from trial attorneys when asked why they oppose banning contingent fees and the "no loser pays" feature from the U.S. tort system.

What you are likely to hear is that those features give the "little guy" access to a legal system that might otherwise be unaffordable, along with the ability to fight the "big guy" without financial intimidation.

If that is the only rationale supporting those features, it isn't nearly good enough when weighed against the extreme harm caused by the *the lawsuit lottery* it encourages.

What the trial lawyers claim they want—assuming they mean what they say—can be achieved largely by alternate means, *without harming the civil justice system*. Indigents, for instance, have a variety of ways of obtaining legal assistance without joining in a financial partnership with personal injury attorneys.

How is it done elsewhere in the world? It's not!

In England, for example, lawyers for the most part are *banned* from working on a contingent fee basis, nor are contingent fees allowed anywhere else in the modern world. Instead, lawyers are required to bill by the hour for work performed. If a client's complaint has merit, the attorney accepts the case and collects a fee from any proceeds that may result from the lawsuit, which typically include legal fees paid by the loser.

The beauty of this approach is that it requires lawyers to carefully examine each case and ensure that it has merit before taking it to court. The objective is to inject justice into lawsuits not just increase their number.

While the elimination of contingent fees is highly unlikely at the present time, reforms could be put in place that would significantly reduce the unhealthy lawyer-client financial partnership that currently exists in most civil lawsuits. This could be accomplished by limiting allowable fees and encouraging the legal profession to bill for services by the hour.

Equally unlikely is the prospect of scrapping the present "no loser pays" system. Even so, judges should be encouraged to awards fees and costs more often to the winners of legal disputes. Such a trend would discourage frivolous litigation and force plaintiffs' attorneys to more seriously evaluate the merit of cases before filing them in the *lawsuit lottery.*

Taken together these two reforms would help rehabilitate the image of today's lawyers, while enhancing the public's respect for the law.

JUDICIAL REFORM

Court reform is as important as tort reform in returning Justice to America's civil justice system. Judges must remember that courts are places where injured people can be compensated for wrongs done to them—not where opportunists can strike it rich!

Unless judges get back in the business of judging the merit of cases instead of merely assigning blame, little change in America's lawsuit mentality can be expected.

First and foremost, judges should reinstate the "reasonable man" and "assumption of risk" standards in determining fault.

If a person knows or should know that something is obviously dangerous or problematic, it stands to reason that no one else should be held responsible if that inherent danger or problem results in an injury to the complaining person. Why, for instance, should a woman who spills hot coffee on herself while in a car be entitled to collect $600,000 from the retailer who sold that container of coffee? The legal logic behind that judgment and myriad others like it boggles the mind.

Another wacky feature that should be discarded by the courts where it still exists is the concept of "joint and several liability," which makes no sense at all.

Why should trial attorneys be able to cause someone with no more than, say, a 5% liability to pay as much as 50% or more of a judgment simply because that defendant has pockets deep enough to do so? Where's the justice in that? Fortunately, efforts are underway to roll back this decidedly unjust plaintiff-favoring tactic. Thankfully, many states have already either eliminated or significantly limited the circumstances in which the doctrine of "joint and several liability" can be employed.

Judges must once again exert their authority to decide which cases get their day in court. The objective here is to eliminate frivolous lawsuits that bog down the system and drive up its cost. Judges must begin identifying frivolous lawsuits early on, disposing of them quickly with summary judgments.

Where the nature of the disputes warrant and where the law permits, judges also should be willing to order independently administered mediation and/or arbitration to help settle disagreements fairly and expeditiously without tying up the courts with costly and protracted litigation.

Other dubious cases also would soon disappear if the courts opted to enforce the existing rule requiring plaintiffs to pay miscellaneous expenses advanced by their attorneys. There was a case in England, for example, where a patient sued a doctor for $350, claiming the physician gave the patient a cold during a physical examination. The presiding judge dismissed the complaint and ordered the patient to pay $1,500 in costs. It wouldn't take too many of those cases to whittle down the overwhelming number of frivolous lawsuits clogging the courts today.

Unfortunately, lawyers in this country prefer to absorb such miscellaneous expenses, not out of kindness but out of fear that to do otherwise might drive away potential contingent fee clients.

Civil court judges also should strive to bring civility back to every courtroom in America. They can help do this by sanctioning attorneys for any perceived abuses, such as unethical practices, bullying tactics and otherwise rambunctious behavior.

The American Bar Association and state bar associations should do the same by upgrading their rules, making them as tough as they used to be—and by enforcing them vigorously.

There is also an important role in the tort reform process to be played by the nation's law schools.

Greater law school emphasis on ethics in the *practice* of law is needed, not just concern about keeping client accounts straight and making certain client money is never co-mingled with the lawyer's. One semester of class work on a topic as important as ethics just won't cut it.

AVOIDING OVERKILL

As with any attempt at major reform, care should always be taken to ensure that the pendulum of legislative and judicial change does not swing too far the opposite way—as it did 50 years ago when those in authority came to believe that long ignored moral and social problems, such as discrimination and workers' rights, could be solved through freewheeling litigation.

What we got as a result of that sea change in law, according to Philip K. Howard, was *a la carte* justice, where the selfish wants of individuals eventually took precedence over the rights of society.

Ignored was what history teaches about the dangers of reform, namely, that we may become too dedicated to it and engage in overkill.

The great French painter Eugene Delacroix put it this way: "Experience has two things to teach: the first is that we must correct a great deal; the second is that we must not correct too much." Delacroix's words hold no less truth or significance when applied today to the desperately needed reform of the much abused and abusive U.S. tort system.

Having said that, however, none should confuse the passion of arguments offered in favor of system reform with any desire to see individuals that harm society not held to account, or to leave industries free to pollute or otherwise destroy the environment, or to allow corporations to sell unsafe products, or to impede anyone with a legitimate grievance from having access to real justice based on the *Rule of Law*.

To the contrary, this commentary is about reforming the *excesses* of a tort system gone terribly bad—about establishing reasonable and responsible restraints on what may be litigated in today's courts and what should be dismissed as frivolous or consigned to other less costly and more expeditious forums for dispute resolution, such as mediation and/or arbitration.

Some of the suggestions offered here already have succeeded in garnering sufficient support for the enactment of tort reform on a piecemeal basis throughout the country. Others have not.

Where there has been success, there must be reinforcement. Where success has been elusive, pressure for reform must be applied again and again until a critical mass of national support is finally achieved.

In the end, the system must change—one way or another. The question is how and when? If nothing is done, the U.S. tort system will fall of its own dead weight, with lawyers, judges and plaintiffs scurrying frantically out from under the crash. If nothing is done, there most assuredly will be a day of reckoning—a breaking point when fear of the system will outweigh the corruption that now envelops it. And what a day that will be!

It will be a day in which the most cynical of all anti-lawyer jokes will prove not to be so cynical after all. "How many lawyer jokes are there? Only one. All the rest are true stories."

CITIZEN REFORM

In the last analysis, the best hope for reform of the U.S. tort system is through grassroots citizen reform—by fundamental change in those public attitudes that have become infected by the growing sense of victimization and entitlement that fuels *the lawsuit lottery* today.

Unless and until the public decides to abandon its lawsuit mentality, the likelihood of any meaningful tort system reform and a return to judicial sanity is little to none.

Of course, if the disastrous economic effects of *the lawsuit lottery* grow much worse, politicians may have no choice but to make changes in the U.S. tort system—just as they did in Mississippi when the medical establishment threatened to move out of that tort-friendly state unless reasonable caps were put on tort liability.

The danger is that politicians may wait too long to get the message and that by then draconian measures may be needed. The other danger, of course, is that if they wait that long, there may be nothing left to save of the *Rule of Law* or the civil justice system. Then what?

Needed is a return to the attitudes that helped this nation grow great when self-interest was the exception and not the rule, as it appears today, and where personal accountability and responsibility were the hallmarks of America's age of rugged individualism.

As Charles J. Sykes suggests in his book, *A Nation of Victims*, "Recognizing our own responsibility and the need to stop blaming others is the first step toward dismantling the culture of victimization." Sykes went on to say, "It's time to drop the crutch."

A recent *Newsweek* story, entitled "Lawsuit Hell," was equally blunt about the public's need to grow up and stop whining about every complaint:

"The time may come when ordinary American citizens recognize that for every sweepstakes winner in the legal lottery, there are millions of others who have to live with the consequences—higher taxes and insurance rates, educational and medical systems seriously warped by lawsuits, fear and uncertainty about getting sued themselves. One day, they may realize that their right to sue has become a trial for all of us."

Unlike changes in legislative and judicial reform, changes in public attitudes cannot be mandated. They must be developed through steady, effective communications reinforced continually and nurtured over time. The difficulty, as Catherine Crier, former lawyer and judge and now TV commentator, points out in her book, *The Case Against Lawyers*, is that America, with its great melting pot of hyphenated diversity, has become a quarrelsome culture, where individuals rule supreme, accountable to no one but themselves, without a sense of public or social responsibility.

In her book, Crier likens America's national character to "Balkan pluralism... wherein our differences are utmost and our unity almost nonexistent...." She goes on to say, "Our increasing diversity has produced no shared acceptance of right and wrong, yet agreed goals and responsibilities are essential to a free but ordered society."

All of this bodes poorly for any quick reversal of the public's deepening propensity for selfish entitlement. In a very real sense, the damage to America's individual and collective character from the abdication of personal responsibility is a self-inflicted wound, very real and likely to fester more before it has any chance of healing. That healing is not likely to occur, however, until such time as Americans come to understand that by punishing each other through *the lawsuit lottery,* we ultimately punish ourselves.

Even when we think we win, we lose.

There is an old saying that relates to these circumstances very well. "When wealth is lost, nothing is lost; when health is lost, something is lost; when character is lost, all is lost!"

Kahlil Gibran saw the problem from a somewhat different perspective and wrote about it in *The Prophet* almost a hundred years ago:

> "The murdered is not unaccountable for his own murder, and the robbed is not blameless in being robbed. The righteous is not innocent of the deeds of the wicked, and the white-handed is not clean in the doings of the felon. Yea, the guilty is oftentimes the victim of the injured. And still more often the condemned is the burden bearer for the guiltless and the unblamed.
>
> "You cannot separate the just from the unjust and the good from the wicked; for they stand together before the face of the sun even as black thread and the white are woven together."

... For Justice in the World

"No man is an Island, entire of itself; every man is a piece
of the Continent, a part of the main..."

—"Meditation XVII" by John Donne (1572–1631)
English poet

A final word about *The Lawsuit Lottery*. When this book was conceived over four years ago, we had no idea that the primary focus of our life would not be the practice of law, and the running of a successful business. We were knee deep in life, like most of us are when there is a business to run, families to attend to, and kids on the way. As this book goes to press in the summer of 2004, the out-of-control legal system that is its subject seems now just a reminder of far greater needs in a "world gone mad."

Today we spend well over half of our time in developing countries in Africa, the Caribbean, and South America. The practice of law, which was once simply our ticket to financial freedom, has in fact become far more important as a funding source for international aid and development. We find ourselves in a new class of social entrepreneurs, which we didn't even know existed, made up of people who see their role in society extending far beyond the traditional boundaries of family and immediate community.

In 2002 we created *World Children's Relief & Volunteer Organization, Inc.*, a 501(c)(3) non-profit charity empowered to offer real hope through education to some of the 130 million children in the world who have been deprived of it.

Initially we were motivated by a sense of social responsibility to share what we had been given the opportunity to earn. We soon learned that in the process of sharing what we earned, we were getting something far greater than we ever imagined in return.

As we traveled the world reviewing our programs and their locations to ensure we were "responsible" in our giving, something else happened. We began touching the lives of children, hearing their stories and their dreams. We were opening ourselves to a world we never knew existed, a world of unbelievable faith, hope and unconditional love.

The children didn't understand our world of business, politics and all the concerns of modern industrialized life. They understood only that we were there. They gave their love without thought, knowing that we would receive it as purely as it was given. There was no agenda, only unfettered joy in the fact that we had come to see them, to share a few moments together and let them know we cared.

As we write about this today, it is hard to imagine ever going back to what our lives used to be. The day we chose to look away from our desks, stacked high as they always were with important business papers, and open our hearts and minds to the real beauty, and the real pain, of this world, it was as if our eyes suddenly could see something that was always there but had gone unnoticed.

For years our sole mission was to serve our clients with the highest standard of care and to protect them and their assets from unjustified attack in a legal system that seemed corrupted in every sense of the word. While our law firm continues providing the same high standard of legal care for thousands of clients today, our personal mission has taken on a much greater purpose.

Today we hope to share the gift those children have given us with our clients and all of us who sometimes get so caught up in what we are doing at the office that we forget to "look up from our desks." To do this, we have created an international volunteer program that provides opportunities for us all to see these children and to feel firsthand the great joy we have experienced.

We no longer see giving as an obligation, forced upon us by the great imbalance and need in the world. We see it instead as an opportunity and the source of our greatest pleasure. That pleasure is the gift of unconditional love we receive every time we are fortunate enough to be a giver. The wonder of it all is that we all have the same opportunity, at some point in our lives, to discover that very same gift of joy that comes with being a truehearted giver.

Douglass S. Lodmell   Benjamin R. Lodmell
Co-Founder   *Co-Founder, Executive Director*

For more information about *WCR*, you can write to *World Children's Relief & Volunteer Organization, Inc.*, 400 E. Van Buren, Suite 850, Phoenix, AZ 85004 or call (602) 288-2596. Or contact us via the web at *www.worldchildrensrelief.org* or by e-mail at *info@worldchildrensrelief.org*.

About World Children's Relief

The vision of *World Children's Relief & Volunteer Organization, Inc.* is to give all children the opportunity to reach their full potential through instilling in them self-respect, dignity and the belief that hope is real.

The primary means to achieving this goal is through the adoption of established and government-recognized primary schools in poor, rural areas of developing countries. *WCR* implements educational programs into these schools that will secure a balanced and quality education for the rural poor.

Named the *Leon H. Sullivan Schools for Education & Self-Help*, this network of early childhood development and primary schools is a symbol of the possibilities of poor children and unlocks their incredible potential, increasing our expectations of them and their own expectations of themselves.

World Children's Relief & Volunteer Organization is based in Phoenix, Arizona.

About World Connection Publishing

World Connection Publishing is an independent, non-profit publishing company dedicated to providing opportunity for emerging artists, writers, painters, photographers, film directors and musicians with a focus on social commentary and world humanitarian interests.

By empowering emerging artists from developing countries and promoting cultural exchanges from around the world, *World Connection Publishing* builds intercultural respect for a more peaceful world.

As a non-profit publishing company, profits made from the sale of *The Lawsuit Lottery: The Hijacking of Justice in America* will be donated to *World Children's Relief,* a non-profit charity founded by the authors.

World Connection Publishing is based in Phoenix, Arizona.